Bobby Allison
A Racer's Racer

www.SportsPublishingLLC.com

Publisher: **Peter L. Bannon**
Senior Managing Editor: **Susan M. Moyer**
Art Director: **K. Jeffrey Higgerson**
Developmental Editor: **Doug Hoepker**
Interior Graphic Designers: **K. Jeffrey Higgerson, Jackie Hettinger**
Cover Graphic Designer: **Christine Mohrbacher**
Copy Editor: **Cynthia L. McNew**

Audio

Kencom Productions, Inc., Mooresville, NC: Narration written and recorded by
Tim Packman; audio production by Clint Wiles. All music, recording, editing,
mixing and CD pre-mastering by Steve Richards of Performance Racing Network.

Photography

Front cover photo: ©Bettmann/CORBIS
Back cover photo: Dick Conway
All interior photos courtesy of Bobby Allison except where noted.
Interior photos by Dick Conway: 2, 71, 74, 79, 105, 107, 111, 115, 122, 123, 127
Interior photos ©Bettmann/CORBIS: 113
Interior photos by AP/WWP: 13, 16, 34, 77, 87, 92

www.SportsPublishingLLC.com
ISBN: 1-58261-723-6
Printed in the United States

Dedication

To the memory of my dad, Edmond Jacob Allison, Sr., who gave me the work ethic that contributed so strongly to my success. "You must do your best every day," he would say. And he helped Davey and Clifford to do the things they should do properly to advance their careers.

To my mom, Kitty Allison, who always supported all of us.

To my sons, Davey and Clifford.

To my daughters, Bonnie and Carrie, who've always been there for me.

To Judy, for being my loving wife and the mother of our children—Davey, Bonnie, Clifford and Carrie.

To Ralph Stark, Al Gorham and Bo Fields for their great support through the years.

And, of course, to all the great fans through the years from Spokane, Washington to Key West, Florida—thanks for enjoying this with me.

—Bobby Allison

To my best friend and loving wife, Dawn, for being there for me and for allowing me to live out my dream of playing with race cars. And for just putting up with me.

To her son, Justin, for listening to me babble on about playing with race cars.

To my dad, Dick Packman, for being my first racing hero and teaching me so much about life.

To my mom, Diana Hayn, for sharing a passion for sports and pointing the way.

To my brother Jim for being the best and my sisters Cheryl and Jerilyn for sharing the love of laughter in life. And to the rest of my family for their love.

To my stepfather, Jim Jividen, for being a racing hero and supporting my endeavors.

To Gary R., Warren B., Dave W., Rich B., John D., Mike D., Scott B., Leslie S., Tony M., Howie M. and Pete T. for defining what friendship truly means.

To the fans in the stands at Lancaster Speedway in Buffalo, NY., especially the Turn One Gang.

Most of all, to my favorite person in the whole world, my grandmother Jane Broker, for her love and guidance.

—Tim Packman

Audio Table of Contents

Table of Contents

Foreword

I first met Bobby Allison back in the early 1970s when he raced his short-track cars at a lot of short tracks I raced, too. He'd put on a great show for the fans. He always helped me and talked to the guys at those races.

I ended up going down to Bobby's home in Hueytown, Alabama, and buying one of his short-track cars. It was a Pontiac Ventura, and we turned it into a Grand National car. We took it to Daytona, where it ran real well, but we blew an engine in the race.

Through thick and thin, Bobby has been a really good friend of mine. Whenever I was in trouble with a bad-handling car, I could always call him and ask for a suggestion. He was the first one to call me back and give me a hand.

Along with my father, Russell, Bobby's always been a hero of mine because he's always been a first-class racer. Bobby is a nuts-and-bolts racer, and he knew his cars in and out. He wasn't a driver who just drove the car; he knew a lot about them.

Bobby knew how to design the cars, and he could handle himself in a great way. He was controversial at times with the sanctioning body of NASCAR. He just wouldn't put up with some of the things they wanted him to do when he knew it was wrong. He would be very boisterous and talk about it, too.

People always ask me who my hero is in racing, and I tell them it's Bobby Allison. He has taught me so much about race cars, how to run up front, and how to win races.

As far as Tim Packman authoring this book with Bobby, Bobby made a good choice. There are a lot of good things to say about

Tim as a writer and a person. He's a good friend of mine and has always been very fair when writing about me and everyone else. He has a great passion and respect for racing and those in the sport.

One thing many people don't know is that he's a good track announcer, too. We used to listen to him when my son, Stephen, was racing and winning all those Bandalero races at the inner track of Lowe's Motor Speedway. Tim is a real quality person, and I'm glad Bobby did this book and CD with him.

As far as Bobby Allison telling a story, why wouldn't people want to hear about this man's life on and off the track? He has been to so many tracks around the country. He won the Daytona 500 three times and notched a victory at almost every track where NASCAR has run races.

Bobby's an absolute legend and is one of the most savvy drivers, hardest chargers and toughest competitors I have ever known. He is a world-class racer and has been there and done it—and probably won it, too.

Whether it was the designing end, the public relations end or Victory Lane, Bobby has been there and done it, several times over. If you want to learn something about racing, you should read this book and listen to what Bobby has to say.

—Rusty Wallace

Acknowledgments

As my recovery from the accident at Pocono in 1988 has continued and I've improved, I've thought a lot about the different things that went on in my life. There have been many really neat things that have happened to me.

I haven't really had a chance to compile those memories in one place like we have done in this book. So I thought it would be a lot of fun to do the book and CD in this format. Writing this book has allowed me to take another look at some of the things that have happened in my life—both on the track and off—and share them with you.

This is a great way for friends and fans to rekindle their memories and enjoy these moments for a second time. A lot of you enjoyed them when they happened, but this book gives you the opportunity to go back over those moments in print, a second time. I hope it all comes back to you as you read or hear about the memories captured in this book, and I hope you get a real big kick out of it, too.

For fans who are new to racing, you are always so interested in the history of this sport. I feel that some things that went on with myself and others from the early days helped the popularity and growth of the sport and really helped build the strong base that NASCAR enjoys today.

A lot of that came from some of the stories that were told in this book. I hope you enjoy them as much as I have enjoyed telling them.

Bobby Allison

Bobby Allison

Introduction

What you are about to read is truly a labor of love.

A love for a sport I was raised on around the short tracks of Western New York. A love for a father and stepfather who raced. A love for an uncle who was a starter at almost every track in the same area. A love for a mother who taught me it was okay to have a favorite, but to still cheer for the other guys, too.

This labor of love comes from wanting to know the details and stories about the history of my sport—racing.

Whether it was a Modified knock-down drag-out at Lancaster Speedway, a Late Model show down at Holland Speedway, or a Street Stock fender banger at Perry Raceway, I wanted to know who was involved, why it happened and how it turned out. And after more than three decades of being around speedways, I'm still that way.

My first direct contact with Bobby Allison came during Speedweeks at Daytona International Speedway in 1995. I had snuck—yes, snuck—into the garage area using a partial pass. There's a fenced walkway between the NASCAR Winston Cup and NASCAR Busch Series garages that leads to the owner/driver motorcoach lot.

I just happened to be there when I saw Bobby Allison come walking through. He seemed 20 feet tall to me. He was just walking along in jeans and a checked shirt looking like an ordinary person sauntering through.

But it was Bobby Allison—the 1983 NASCAR Winston Cup Series Champion, winner of 85 races (84, according to NASCAR's record book), three-time winner of the Daytona 500, and a fan favorite for years. He's a founder of the famous Alabama Gang and either won or took part in some of the best battles in NASCAR history. He's survived more in one lifetime than some families have endured through generations. And he is one of my four favorite drivers of all time.

Without flinching, I pulled out my pad and pen and asked "Mr. Allison" for an autograph. He stopped and must have seen the dazed wonderment in my eyes. He raised his hands shoulder high as if he was going to say "Son, I don't have time for that right now," and move on. But instead, he said, "Look, you have to understand something." Fear went through my entire body—what had I said wrong? Was there something I wasn't aware of?

I froze.

"Son, you have to understand something," as he lowered his chin to the side, but kept his eyes on mine. "I went to night school and I don't write too well during the day," he said with a grin.

My head snapped up and I smiled brighter than the Florida sun at midday. I was talking with Bobby Allison for the first time in my life—and he cracked a joke! Relieved and uneasy at the same time, I thanked him and briskly walked away. I don't know where I was going, but I was getting there pretty darn fast because I had to show that autograph to someone and tell them the story!

It would be five more years before I would get the chance to talk with Bobby, but it was well worth the wait. My career path took me from Buffalo, New York, to the shores of the Gulf of Mexico in Treasure Island, Florida, back to Buffalo, and finally, to my dream destination of Mooresville, N.C., as a writer at NASCAR.com.

At the time, it was the end of the 2000 season and Darrell Waltrip was retiring after the season finale at Atlanta Motor Speedway. We were asking many drivers who raced against Waltrip through the years to share their related memories. Thinking this was my chance to formally interview Bobby, I tracked down his whereabouts from Hueytown, Alabama, to—now get this—five miles from where I lived.

I got his home number and nervously called to get his thoughts about the event. He answered and I politely introduced myself, said where I was calling from and that I wanted to get some quotes from him on the aforementioned event.

His reply to me that Friday afternoon was, "Let me think about it and get back to you." He must have great things he wanted to tell me; or so I thought.

While driving home that night, it hit me like a lead-pack draft at Daytona coming off turn four for the checkered flag. "Bobby probably doesn't want to talk about that topic and was politely telling me to go jump off a bridge when I called," was my thought.

For the whole weekend, I fretted that I had hurt his feelings or upset him, and it bothered me to no end. On Monday, I called him to say I was sorry I asked him to talk about the topic and that I was just so happy to have a reason to talk with him, and that I should have given it more thought, and he realized what happened and he apologized, too.

What could have been a wreck turned into a great run. I then came up with the idea of talking to inactive racers (they never really retire) for a series about what they were up to now, and I asked Bobby to be my first interview. He not only said yes, but he invited me over to his house to conduct the interview. I offered up lunch afterwards, and he readily accepted.

That first official meeting between Bobby Allison and me lasted three hours, and I swore it was like 10 minutes. He talked about his uneasiness in discussing that matter with me, and I readily understood when he was done.

Then he launched into story after story about things that happened to him, how he met his wife Judy (she has her own version of this story that's on the CD), racing with his son Davey, what his son Clifford was like, his fateful accident in 1988, and a variety of other topics. I walked out of that house not only feeling like the luckiest person in the world, but also blessed that I heard those stories from the source himself—Bobby Allison.

This book delves into some of the serious, funny, lighter and downright forthcoming things that Bobby has experienced during his lifetime. As I ran into Bobby at other racing functions, I was truly amazed at how people are drawn to this man. But at the same time, I wasn't really surprised. People remember every car he drove, where he drove it, where he won, and the times that they also had met him in person.

Then again, I just told you every detail of the first time I met Bobby, too. So I guess I fit into that category.

Having been around Bobby socially and at racing functions, I have always been mesmerized by how he tells a story. The way his voice trails off for a minute, then picks up to restore your interest is intriguing. When he pauses, he'll raise his hands to shoulder height in front of his chest and say, "Now, wait a minute," before continuing.

One day, while I was listening to that original interview from the winter of 2000, the thought occurred to me that these stories needed to be told. Sure, most fans can tell about Bobby and some of the things that have happened to him. But can anyone tell it better than the man who actually sat in the driver's seat of his own life? I think not.

Let this book and CD be something you enjoy as Bobby tells the tales, trials and tribulations of his life—in his own words. Racing was a labor of love for this champion among champions, and his passion to win was his engine.

Bobby, you have inspired me to never forget where the sport came from—who was there or how it happened. History is something we can't change, but we can grow from learning about it as we move forward. I grow every time I get to read or hear about the history of our sport.

Bobby, this book is also a labor of love for you, your inspiration and determination. And for that, I say thank you, my friend. You are truly *A Racer's Racer.*

—Tim Packman

1979 Daytona 500

When CBS Sports said they were going to broadcast the first NASCAR race from start to finish live on their network, the skeptics rained down upon them. To the network's advantage was the fact Mother Nature also did the same—but in the form of snow.

With most of the Northeast socked in by bad weather, and only three networks available nationwide at the time, the casual and devout sports fans tuned into this NASCAR race to see what it was all about. Not only did they see history in television, but they saw a historic finish in NASCAR that is still talked about today.

Bobby Allison, his brother Donnie Allison and Cale Yarborough slugged it out—literally—at the end of the "Great American Race". And, the cameras of CBS caught the action blow by blow.

I won the Daytona 500 the year before in my first year with Bud Moore. We had a pretty good year, winning a total of five races. And, here we were back in Daytona for the 500 for the second go around. I guess we weren't nearly as good, speed wise, as we were the year before. But, I was still pretty confident about the situation.

This is the last-lap wreck that started it all in the 1979 Daytona 500.

AP/WWP

We started the race somewhere in the front stages of the pack. We got going early and of course the car would drive good and draft good, and I was in the thick of things pretty quickly. I would always jump in there and draft with people and enjoyed that type of thing and did pretty good with it.

So, Donnie, Cale and I were running pretty close to the front. Donnie was leading, and I was in there drafting with him and Cale was, too. Somebody got a little out of shape and the three of us got together and went spinning into the infield grass on the back straightaway. We went spinning down in there, and I got stuck in the mud and so did Cale. Donnie got going again and Cale and I ended up a couple of laps behind. My day was pretty well used up.

I was plugging along doing the best I could and Donnie was out there leading the race. He quickly got back to the front and really had the dominant car. Cale could draft with Donnie but couldn't pass him. They were running with Donnie leading and Cale two laps behind. The yellow flag came out and Donnie backed off and Cale got one of his laps back.

Donnie didn't think much of it, he thought Cale was more than two laps behind. The race continues with Donnie leading and Cale back there drafting along with him when the yellow came out again. Donnie backed off, and Cale got by him and got his other lap back. Now Cale was on the lead lap.

So, I'm going along there and, by then, we had pretty good radio communications. My crew radioed me and told me I was coming to take the white flag and that Donnie and Cale were really going at it, so give them plenty of room. I was going to go in the infield if I had to, but I could see they were a good ways behind me. As I entered Turn 3, the caution lights came on. I still hadn't taken the white flag so I had to race back to the caution. I got the white flag and came around and saw all this wreckage.

It was really bad, but Donnie was already climbing out of his car. I was relieved he wasn't hurt in any bad way. My job was to finish the race, so I went around and got the checkered flag. I went back around and slowed down to the area and the two cars were probably 75-100 feet apart with a few safety guys around Cale and a few around Donnie.

I pulled down on the track, closer to Donnie's car, because they were off in the grass. I called out to Donnie and asked if he wanted a ride back to the garage. He said to go on and that he would find a ride. So, I put the car in gear to head for the garage area, and Cale started yelling that the wreck was my fault.

Of course, the way I have to tell that particular part of the story is that I'm sure I questioned his ancestry. With that, Cale jumped up and waved his fist at me with his helmet in his hand. He started running, still yelling and blaming me for the wreck. I think I questioned his ancestry a little further.

He got closer to the car and I thought for sure he was going to stop and just yell some more. That was the deal back in those days, a lot of guys yelled and that was the end of the deal. Well, he lunged at me and hit me in the face with his helmet. It really surprised me. It stunned me and hurt.

I looked down in my lap and there were a few droplets of blood. I said to myself, "I have to get out of this car and address this right now or run from him the rest of my life." So, I got out of the car. And, with that, Cale went to beating on my fist with his nose.

That's my story—and I'm sticking to it.

Here's a shot of the famed ending to the 1979 Daytona 500 where Cale Yarborough went to beating on my fist with his face. Notice the track worker "trying" to separate us.

AP/WWP

Fine Way to Finish a Race

When the race was over, Richard Petty had taken the checkered flag, and NASCAR went on to take something from Bobby, Donnie, and Cale. According to Bobby, they got the better end of the deal from that historic 1979 Daytona 500 finish.

After that fight, we scrambled around there for a little bit, and the safety crews all grabbed us. There are pictures with Donnie holding a helmet like he's swinging it at Cale. Well, what Donnie was saying was, "I have a helmet, too. If you want to fight with helmets, I can fight that way, too." He never hit Cale a lick or confronted him in any way. It ended up being me and Cale.

So after the race I went on home. NASCAR called and said they had decided to fine me $6,000—it just floored me! That was a gigantic fine. I had just finished 11th, and the winnings were about $17,000, of which only half of that ($8,500) was mine. Now NASCAR said they were going to keep $6,000 of that.

But the bottom line of that whole story is that NASCAR's part of the purse didn't cover the whole $6,000. So I had to come up with the difference out of my pocket, because they said they needed the check the next day.

I felt like a real victim.

My First Races and Win No. 1

Bobby didn't just stumble into racing; he was introduced to it like a lot of us—by a family member. His grandfather took a young Bobby to the races one night, and as they say, the rest is history, in more ways than one.

His eagerness to get to the track, his passion to race, and his penchant for winning started at a young age. And it continued through four decades of his legendary life.

I was a race fan ever since I was a kid. My grandfather—my mom's dad—lived with us, and he was a sports fan. He wasn't an athlete, but he was a sports fan. He went to all kinds of events. He would go to football, baseball, roller derbys and such. He would take one of us 10 children as a companion.

Here I am on my tricycle at five years old in 1943. See, I'm already racing.

One night, he told me he was going to the car races and wanted to know if I wanted to go along. I thought, "Sure, that would be great," and off we went to the old Opolacka (Florida) Speedway. It was built on the old Naval Air Station supply area. They had all these paved lanes that were parallel, and they put dirt turns down there. So you had this track with paved straightaways and dirt turns.

This was wild and the greatest thing I had ever seen in my life—at the age of 10, anyhow. From there, I bugged my grandfather, dad, anyone in the neighborhood to take me to the races. Pretty soon, they paved the corners, and that made it better yet.

Then they built Hialeah (Florida) Speedway. By then, I was old enough to ride my motorcycle to the races, because you could get a motorcycle license

Hanging out on the front lawn of my house in Miami when I was all of 12 years old.

at age 14. So you know on my 14th birthday I had my little Mustang motorcycle, and I would go to the races. I was really into them.

They decided to have this Amateur Division. I had this '38 Chevy Coupe that I was driving to school. Luckily, it had a straight axle, which wasn't great for a ride, but it did handle very well. I found out that you had to have a parent's permission if you were under 18 years old.

I went to my mom, Miss Kitty, because I figured it would be easier to finesse her than my dad for this written permission. Dad was a neat guy, but he worked all the time, had us 10 kids and really had to be on the go all the time. He didn't put up with any foolishness and wasn't easy to negotiate with.

Here's Judy's "boyfriend" after winning a race in his 1934 Chevy Sedan at Hialeah (Florida) Speedway in 1954.

So I went to Mom and told her I just had to race. She said no, that she wanted me to go to college to be a doctor, a lawyer—whatever. I told her that I had to race and that it was going to be good. Well, I told her if she gave me permission to race, I would improve my grades. I promised her, and it was a done deal. She wrote me out the permission, and I went off to race.

There were about 30 cars there the first night, and I finished seventh. I thought that was pretty good. A lot of those guys had better cars and were older than me. The next week, I worked on my car, and there were 40 cars there. I was a little taken aback, but I still went out and finished seventh again. The third week there were 50 cars there—there were cars everywhere. In the parking lot, in the pits and everywhere. Fifty cars started that race, and I won the race.

It was like I won the Indy 500. We didn't have Daytona back then, so it really was a thrill for me.

I kept busy, doing my racing and my schooling and so forth. Well, Mom decided that wasn't what she really wanted for me and thought she had given me written permission for just one week. I thought it was for 100 years—and my deal was working.

This is me and my 1955 Chevy Late Model Modified at Birmingham in 1963. How do you like that driving uniform?

Yachting, Anyone?

om's sister Patty and brother-in-law Jimmy Hallet lived in Wisconsin. Uncle Jimmy was the national sales manager for Mercury Outboard Motors. So she called up Uncle Jimmy, whom I had met a few times when he visited Florida and kept in touch with through letters and such. They said to come on up to Wisconsin, because it would get me away from this racing in Florida.

I said I would come up, but not to visit—I wanted to work. I jumped in a truck they had taking motors to Wisconsin from a boat show and got a free ride up to Wisconsin. Well, he got me a job up there riding around in a boat with an outboard motor on the lakes and rivers of Wisconsin.

And they gave me a paycheck on Friday. Now, this was really the deal. Here it was, the beginning of summer, and I had just graduated high school. Man, what a neat deal. And every little town in Wisconsin had a race track.

Now, I didn't get to race any in Wisconsin then, but I got to go and watch races and watch how different people handled competition. That was pretty neat.

When winter came, I headed back down to Florida, because everything closed up up there. I was in Sarasota when Karl Kiekhaefer drafted me to be a mechanic on his Grand National team, which was in Charlotte at the time. I worked on cars for Buck Baker, Speedy Thompson, Jimmy Thompson, Jack Smith, Herb Thomas— he had a whole stable of drivers.

I learned about setups, preparation and how to make things reliable. That was a good education for me.

Here's me (second from left) and some friends hanging out on the beach in Sarasota, Florida when I worked for Karl Kiekhaefer's race team.

5 Bobby Allison vs. Bobby Sunderman

When Bobby returned to his home in southern Florida, his mom still wasn't too hip on him racing. Adding to the deal was his dad telling him he couldn't live at home if he was going to race. So being the resourceful person he is, Bobby just changed a little something so he could have it both ways.

Did he fool his dad? Not one darn bit.

I had a car off to the side that I was going to use for racing. But I wanted to live at home. So I had to think about this. I just figured I would change my racing name. At the time, my oldest sister was engaged to a friend of mine in the neighborhood named Bob Sundman.

Bob Sundman had a racing license, but he didn't drive. His family had a race car, and they were involved in racing. He said, "I'll just let you use my license, and you could use that name." So that was a good deal.

Well, I went to the race track, and the pit steward recognized the deal right off the bat. So he changed the name to Bob Sunderman. He knew I wasn't Bob Sundman, but I couldn't be Bobby Allison. And I raced.

I probably finished fifth or sixth in the feature that night. The next day, there was a real tiny column in the Miami paper that gave the rundown. My dad looked at that, and obviously someone had tipped him off. He said, "Hey boy, look here. If you're going to race, use your own name and not somebody else's. If you're going to do it, do it with honor."

That was my dad's attitude to everything. So we went back to Bobby Allison. Even though "Bob Sunderman" was a real short career, it became a bigger deal as time went on, because they all fantasized about what could have been and how big a thing this could have grown into.

It actually didn't grow very big, but the alias name got me through that big first step, and then I was on my way.

This was my 1955 Chevy that I won a bunch of races with in the early years. Here I am with Chuck Looney (glasses) and another crewman after winning at Birmingham (Alabama) International Raceway in 1963.

I drove this 1936 Chevy Coupe—with fuel injection—for William Mason from Bassett, Va., in a few races in 1963 and won once. His regular driver, "Perk" Brown, was sick.

"Crash" Armstrong—
The Educator

As Bobby's racing interest grew, so did his desire to go faster. In that quest, he decided to build a 1934 Chevy Coupe Modified to take to the short tracks in Florida.

During this time he met a man who was not only very helpful to him regarding the care of his car, but also in nurturing the future NASCAR great.

This old man used to stop by my shop, and he started helping me with my car. His name was Roy Armstrong, and he was just perfect for me at the time. He was delightful to be around—and a great educator.

He had these little sayings that he would give to me along the way. Real early in the situation, some kids came to me at the races and wanted my autograph. They were just down there collecting autographs when the races were over.

I thought, "What do you want mine for?" I got all curious about this and was kind of reluctant. Roy turned to me and said, "Listen here kid, let me tell you. Every request for an autograph is a compliment."

And it still is today.

Roy's greatest lesson to me was, "Listen here kid, every race track has two straightaways and four corners. You have to handle twice as good as you run."

So we worked on the handling, and I really made that my strong suit. He helped me put things together on how you can improve that. He really was my ace in the hole my whole career.

The funny thing about Roy was that he would come by every afternoon after he got off his regular job in one of the construction/iron worker trades. He was kind of an old man to me at the time, at 65 or 70 years old. He had been a Sprint Car racer back in the 1930s on the old dirt tracks.

Well, one afternoon I was really counting on him for something that we were doing. We had talked about it, and so I got concerned when he didn't come over. So I called his house.

He answered, "Yeah, whadya want?" I said, "Roy, what's the matter?" He told me he just had a real bad wreck. "You did? Are you hurt?" I said. "Naw, I'm not hurt, but I tore my little truck all to pieces."

"Roy, what happened?" I asked. "Well, I was going down 32nd Ave. and some guy came through 14th St. and tore my car all to pieces." I said, "Roy, 32nd Ave. is a stop street [lights and stop signs] and 14th St. is a through street [no lights or signs]." Roy replied, "I run that stop street every day at three o'clock, that guy had no business coming through there!"

So I got a big kick out of that, and I gave Roy Armstrong the nickname "Crash." I never called him anything else during our relationship together.

From Peaches to Pay Dirt

During his days in South Florida, Bobby had to work his way through the week to pay his bills because the purses were so sparse. He did this by working on other people's cars.

One day, he dropped an automatic transmission on his hand and tore his hand up pretty bad. After a few hours at the doctors being sewn back up and bandaged, Bobby left there with all his fingers. But he couldn't race for a while.

So I called a friend of mine and got him to run my car, and he did okay. I was really proud of this new car, and we struggled through that deal for nine weeks. At the end of those nine weeks, the doctor told me I could drive again, but I had to use a good glove on my left hand. So I did that.

The first race we had going was a 100-lap feature event on Memorial Day at West Palm Beach. It was a Wednesday night on their half-mile paved oval. Red Farmer won the race, and I finished second.

I was really tickled with that, so I went to the pay window. It was less than $100, it was $95 to finish second—but it was more money than I had ever collected at the pay window.

While I was there, two other youngsters came walking up and said they had been through Georgia and southern Tennessee looking for race tracks. They were Kenny

Andrews and Gil Hearn, who went on to have a pretty decent career in Modifieds in the Northeast.

Gil was the driver, and Kenny was the car owner. They said they didn't find any tracks that were paved; they were all dirt, and they wanted to run paved tracks. They were going to Alabama and asked if I wanted to go, too.

Well, I had all this money. So I went home and told my mom I was going to go to Alabama. She agreed that that's what I probably should do and then said to me, "You should take your brother Donnie with you. I'd appreciate if you'd take your brother with you, because he's driving your dad nuts."

Now, Donnie hates for me to say that part of it, but it was part of the deal. So he got his little suitcase and helmet, because he had some amateur experience. We jumped in my truck with a '34 Modified on a two-wheel trailer behind us, and we headed up the road.

We were going through central Florida and it was right at the beginning of summer, and we passed all these peach stands with beautiful baskets of peaches for 50 cents. And I'm thinking, "Wow, those things look good, and 50 cents is really well within my budget."

Right after I won a race at Nashville in 1964, Louis Workman from Memphis called and asked me to drive this Super Modified the next night. I blew the engine in practice; meanwhile, qualifying and the heat races went on while we installed a new engine. We made the repairs and I started dead last in a 300-lap feature and won the race. I drove this car 11 times during the winter months.

So I told Donnie we would stop and get some peaches and we'd eat peaches for lunch instead of wasting our money on some other kind of food. Donnie agreed, and we stopped and bought a basket of peaches.

We ate peaches for lunch, we ate peaches for supper on Thursday and as a midnight snack, breakfast on Friday was more peaches, and lunch was even more peaches. By now, we were in Alabama. We discovered this state with beautiful highways, nicely groomed area and beautiful countryside. It was very attractive.

So here we were in Alabama. We stopped at a gas station and asked them where we could find the race track. He said there was one 100 miles north in Montgomery, Alabama. So we went around there on the old Southern Bypass, and we saw a race car sitting at a gas station.

When we stopped there, we went in and met Bo Freeman, the owner of the station. Sonny Black was the driver, but Bo was the mechanic on the race car for Sonny. The race car was a 1934 Chevy with a Cadillac V8 and fuel injectors.

Bo was real friendly and said he would take us out to the race track. We followed him out to Montgomery Speedway, and it was a beautiful half-mile track. The promoter came out and told us that they would run the next night, but that Dixie Speedway in Midfield, a suburb of Birmingham, was running that night.

We asked him where it was, and he gave us the directions. After zooming up to Birmingham, we found this pretty little quarter-mile track with nice race cars and a pretty good crowd.

Off we went into there, and I ran fifth in the heat, fifth in the semi-feature and fifth in the feature. So I told Donnie I would head up to the window and get our couple of bucks and go get a hamburger. We were going to stop at the Miss Mary's Drive-In we had passed on the way into the track.

So I got to the pay window, and the man counted me out $135 in a stack of money that looked like it was four inches tall. I said, "Wow!" and headed down the steps of the pay booth yelling, "Donnie, we have died and gone to heaven—look at all this money."

We were going to sleep on the seat of the truck because we were two young guys, we were brothers and we could handle the situation. Well, we ended up going to the drive-in and had one of those $1.98 steaks and slept in a bed that night.

The next day, we went to Montgomery and stopped at Bo's gas station. We were tinkering with the car and wiping it off, waiting for race time to come. I had been advised by several of the fans that hung around Bo's station, which quite a few of them did, not to bring that little Chevy engine to Montgomery, because the Cadillac cars would blow me out into the woods.

My answer to that was, "Well, I've been in the woods before, so I'm going anyway." I went to Montgomery and had a fast time in qualifying, I won the heat race and the semi-feature, and they had an Australian pursuit race. I'd heard of them before, but had never been in one.

It's one of those races where the fastest qualifier starts last, but when you get passed you have to drop out of the race. Well, I ended up winning that race in seven laps.

So then I started on the pole for the feature with Sonny Black to the outside. He was a seasoned racer who had made his living out of bootlegging and racing. He was truly an Alabama character at the time.

He taught me a lesson that helped me win races for the rest of my entire life. He out-accelerated me and pulled down into the bottom lane and would not give me the bottom lane. He forced me to take the top lane, and I couldn't make it by him. He would out-accelerate me on the straightaway, and I couldn't pass him in the corner.

I ended up finishing second, and a lot of people thought I would be really irritated by this deal. But I went to the pay window, and they gave me a stack of money that was way bigger than the one I got the night before. So how could I be mad?

Birth of the Alabama Gang

When race fans talk about the Alabama Gang, there is a sense of reverence. At first consisting of Bobby Allison, Donnie Allison and Red Farmer, the gang grew to include Neil Bonnett and Bobby's son Davey.

The reverence it now evokes was more like defiance when the Alabama Gang first came to fame. And for good reason, when this gang of winners rolled into town.

Donnie and I became residents of Alabama after a while, and I went back to Florida and told my hero, Red Farmer, of the great countryside and tracks and that he should head to Alabama, too. At the time, Red had a little car of his own and had been driving for this car owner who had gotten sick and died. The owner left the car and equipment to Red Farmer in his will. What a way to get into the racing business.

Red was my hero. I told him he needed to be in Alabama. He was in the winning mode, and he just dominated that first year winning like crazy. So he moved to Alabama, and all three of us were racing and doing pretty well at the time.

AP/WWP

The Alabama Gang of Donnie and Bobby Allison with Neil Bonnett in 1977.

Check out these dapper drivers. That's my hero Red Farmer on the lower left. Seated next to Red is Bob Burcham. That's Pat Purcell from NASCAR (far right) with his arm around my shoulder and my brother Donnie behind me.

I saw these special events coming up. One in Memphis, Tennessee, one in Bristol, Tennessee, and places like that. I told them I was going to go to some of these and check them out. So we started campaigning around and going to these events.

Quite often, we would finish first-second-third, and everyone there was fourth or farther on back. We were really in that winning mode, and all three of us ran really good. So we went to the Asheville-Weaverville Speedway one day for a 200-lap Modified race.

As we rolled into the pit area, Jack Ingram—who was a very likeable but very

Turning some laps in my first Late Model Modified (Sportsman) at Birmingham International Speedway in 1963. The car is a real beauty, isn't it?

competitive guy at the time—said, quite loud, "Here comes that dang Alabama Gang." And the moniker just stuck. What a great way to get tabbed the Alabama Gang. By then, Alabama was our home anyway and we were fond of Alabama. To be called the Alabama Gang was just a great compliment to us.

So we just roamed the country as the Alabama Gang.

Then Neil Bonnett became part of the deal in the latter part of the 1970s. When my son, Davey Allison, started racing, he was certainly accepted into the group.

We never had anything to do with it; it's mostly a title put there by the fans. It wasn't done by the rest of the group. You don't join; you don't sign up. For Davey to be inducted into the Alabama Gang by the fans was a real honor to me—and, I'm sure, to Donnie and Red, too.

My brothers Eddie (left) and Donnie (center) helping me work at our shop in Hueytown, Alabama, in 1972.

The Kid Who Wouldn't Go Away

9

Quite a bit later, Neil Bonnett came along and went to work for me. I had heard of him and knew he was racing on some of the tracks around Alabama. I'm not sure how his performance was at the time, but I knew who he was.

I was running my own NASCAR Winston Cup Series car out of my shop in 1977 in Hueytown, Alabama. And working, working and working and not getting stuff done right on this AMC Matador. I was probably a better driver than I was a mechanic, and I was a way better driver than I was an organizer.

I never realized that until the last couple of years. I always thought I was good at everything, but as I look at things there are probably a few things I probably wasn't as good at as I thought.

Here we were trying to run this NASCAR Winston Cup Series car out of this shop in Hueytown. I thought I had pretty decent equipment, but I could not keep my employees on the right track. I ended up in the engine room myself one night at about 8 p.m.

The way my shop was, I would leave my door open. In Alabama, you left a lot of things unlocked anyways. I was there alone, and this guy came in and said he was there to help me—it was Neil Bonnett.

I knew who he was, but I didn't know anything about him. I said, "Look, I'm really busy, I don't need any aggravation, so please leave." He said, "Nope, I'm here and I came to help you, and I'm going to help you."

So I told him I was ready to start building this engine and told him to start cleaning the engine parts. He said okay and jumped in there and did an excellent job. I had paid employees that I had to tell them how to do that. Neil was the greatest helper.

We worked all night. So at about 6:30 a.m., he told me he had to take a shower and go to work and that he had a full-time job. But he said he would be back in the afternoon when he got off of work. I told him I appreciated that, but he didn't need to come back that night because I still had a lot to do.

He left and I went to lie down for a while, slept for a few hours, and went back to work. Neil Bonnett showed back up again, and we got to working away. Well, about midnight we were pretty much caught up on this engine, got it loaded up, and off we went racing.

Neil stayed home, my crew and I went off racing, and I had a fairly decent performance. To have any decent performance is an encouragement. We got back to the shop. Part of the problem was that my employees thought it was a put-down to be working on a lowly Matador instead of a Ford, Chevrolet or a Plymouth.

We got back, and here's Neil Bonnett back asking, "So, what are we going to work on this week?" I told him we had to get ready for the next race, and we worked away. Neil and I

One of the Alabama Gang: Neil Bonnett.

were loading this spare engine to go to Dover, it was like midnight on Thursday, and the truck just had to go out of the driveway no matter what.

The driver was there waiting, so we were hurrying, and we turned the engine stand over on Neil. I was afraid we had broken his legs. It certainly cut him up some, but I was certain a leg was broken. We got this engine off of him, got it loaded in the truck.

I told Neil, "Come on, let me take you to the hospital." He refused and headed on home. Fortunately, it wasn't broken, and he just bandaged it up and went to work at his job the next day.

But that kind of effort was so much of a help to me because his attitude, along with what he could accomplish with his hands, was great. So I asked him what could I do to thank him. He wouldn't take any pay, and I couldn't pay him much anyhow.

He said, "Someday, when you get a chance, I'd like to drive one of your race cars."

This was the original 1964 Chevelle I raced with all over the place. I earned my first three NASCAR wins in this car. This was taken at Daytona in 1966.

"Someday" Becomes "Race Day"

10

Neil Bonnett had been working nights for Bobby at his shop in Hueytown, Alabama, trying to prove his worth. Forgoing sleep to help, Neil never asked Bobby for a dime during this time.

All he asked for was the chance to prove his racing worth in one of Bobby's short-track cars. Remember when Bobby said he was a better driver than he was an organizer? Well, he was right—and that led to Neil's big break in an Allison-built car for the short tracks.

I ended up booking myself into two tracks in one night, and they weren't close to each other. So I told Neil to take one car and go to Smoky Mountain Raceway, in Maryville, Tennessee, promoted by Don Naman. And I told him I'd go to Lonesome Pine Speedway in Coeburn, Virginia.

Neil thought that was fine. But I had to call Don up at Smoky Mountain to tell him I wouldn't be there. So I called Don, and he said, "Oh yeah, good to hear from you, Bobby. Boy, are we looking forward to you being here." I said, "Wait a minute. My car will be there, but Neil Bonnett will be driving it." Don wasn't

Neil Bonnett getting ready for the race at Talladega in 1978 in a car owned by Judy Allison.

too happy. "Nah, nah, you can't do this—Neil who? Neil who?" I told Don, "His name is Neil Bonnett and you will really like him." Don still wasn't too happy, and he replied, "Ah no—you can't do this to me. I'm paying you appearance money and everything." I said, "Don, forget the appearance money. Pay me whatever you think you owe me when the deal is over. Neil Bonnett is going to come, and Neil Bonnett is going to drive the car."

"Aw, you're breaking my heart, Bobby," was what Don said before we hung up.

So I told Neil that I would call him after the race at the speedway office at 11 p.m. from Lonesome Pine and see how he did. I had to go on to my Sunday race the next day. In those days, I was famous for doing the Saturday night deal and being at some NASCAR Winston Cup race event on Sunday.

So at 11 p.m. Saturday night, I called Smoky Mountain Raceway, and Don answered the phone. I said, "Don, this is Bobby Allison." "Oh, you have to promise to send him back next week." I was like, "Whoa, wait a minute, what happened, what did he do?" "Oh, you gotta promise to send him back next week."

I asked Don, "Well, how did he run?" Don said, "You gotta promise to send him back next week." I said, "Don, did he crash?" Again, the response was, "You gotta promise to send him back next week."

Then I said, "Don, did he win?" All Don would say was, "You gotta promise to send him back next week."

"Don, what happened?!" I yelled.

Don proceeded to tell me that Neil Bonnett had captured everybody's heart in Maryville, Tennessee, and what a neat guy he was. I do remember telling Don that he would like him. He then told me the show that Neil put on that night by qualifying on the pole, but he got spun early in the race. He came all the way from last and passed people inside, outside and just had the crowd on their feet and did a great job.

Neil Bonnett receives a trophy after winning the pole at Nashville, Speedway. On the left is Miss Winston, Pattie Huffman, who is now Mrs. Kyle Petty. T. Wayne Robertson is interviewing Neil. I was injured so bad from an earlier wreck that Neil had to qualify the car—where he won the pole—and relieve me (on the far right) after I started the race.

Don said he was going to pay me my appearance fee, but that I had to send Neil Bonnett back next week. Of course I agreed.

From there, Neil and I agreed for him to run some of the short-track races. I was going to line them up for him, run some of the other races with my other car, but mostly concentrate on my NASCAR Winston Cup Series efforts.

Neil drove for me for one and a half years and entered 80 events. He won 60 of them. I could send Neil to a track he had never seen before, which I felt like I could do myself. You follow the black line and turn left. Most people feel like they have to get some familiarity with the track, but Neil didn't.

We got really good at sending Neil to the short tracks, and he'd bring home that purse money. We could then use that to make that Matador go faster.

My First Two NASCAR Winston Cup Wins

Bobby Allison has 85 NASCAR Winston Cup Series wins to his credit. Okay, most places say 84 (including NASCAR's official record book), but we'll explain that a little later. But in order to get to that number, which is third on the all-time win list, you have to win that first one.

Bobby's first and second wins came in just one week's time. Typical over-achieving Allison fashion, too. You have to have some bad luck before you have the good.

A t the time, the series was called the NASCAR Grand National Series. I was winning Sportsman races on a lot of the short tracks and could travel around the country and win at strange places. I had some idea of the Grand National circuit because I had worked for Karl Kiekhaefer as a youngster for two months.

So I had gone by hook or by crook to get a ride here and there and struggled with things. I finally ended up with a car owned by a Mrs. Betty Lilly of Valdosta, Georgia. Sam McQuagge drove for Betty Lilly previously and had won Rookie of the Year in 1965.

The difference was, when Sam drove for Betty Lilly she had a hired mechanic, a hired crew and nice fresh Holman-Moody equipment. Now when it came to me, she said, "Here's the deal, you can drive my car, but I can't pay any of the bills. You have to pay all the bills." I said that was okay. I wanted it so bad that I would do it.

This was the car that Betty Lilly owned and I drove, briefly, in 1966.

So I struggled along with Betty Lilly's car, and it really was a mistake. I finally said one day, "I can't do this." At the time, NASCAR had this rule that the car weight was determined by the size of the engine. We were so successful on the half-mile paved tracks with a little Chevy engine and cars. I built a Chevelle with a little engine, and I went to try and win at the short tracks that NASCAR was running.

I found a 1964 Chevelle in a Birmingham, Alabama, junkyard that had been under water. It had no dents, and everything that was ruined from being under water I had to take out anyway. So my brother Eddie, along with longtime helpers and friends of mine, Chuck Looney and Bo Fields, spent about a week and a half building this Chevelle so we could go race.

Well, the next race on the NASCAR Grand National circuit was in Beltsfield, Maryland. I was familiar with the track because I won there in Modifieds and knew the promoter. I knew I could probably get $50 appearance money, which in those days wasn't bad because there were guys who ran pretty good that didn't get any appearance money.

So I made the deal and headed up there. I ran really good and was leading the race and had a rear-end failure. That was one of those things that happened more than it should have back in those days. But I was out of the race.

Word got out that the car was pretty competitive and pretty attractive. Bill France, Sr. gave me a call and said, "Bobby, the next race is Fourth of July at Daytona. So you go to Junior Johnson's and he has some of those new 427-cubic-inch Chevy engines. Nobody knows that he has them [Junior was a Ford factory racer]. So you go there and get one to put in your car for Daytona on the Fourth of July."

Boy, I got a big smile on my face. I took Chuck with me and went to Junior's shop in North Wilkesboro and installed this 427 Chevy in my little Chevelle. Now as you can imagine, nothing fit.

We built the Chevy thinking small-block style, and boy, what a chore that was. We got this thing all shoved together and got to Daytona. The car was so slow that it was embarrassing to me. I know that my little 327-cubic-inch engine would be a faster race car.

We struggled with it and had a fairly poor finish of 14th, but made it through the event. Then we had to go give the engine back to Junior Johnson. This took up some more of my time, and our best rest was during the days of practice and qualifying, when you had to leave the race track at 5 p.m.

I got back to Junior's and put the little 327-cubic-inch engine back in the car. The next race was at Manassas, Virginia, on what they used to call the Northern Tour. We went there and qualified on the pole and were looking really good. The race report said I had an engine miss, but it was different from what I remembered. I remembered the car quit running and I had a strong smell of gasoline in the car.

I coasted into the infield—it was night and the infield was dark—and stopped. The right floorboard of the car was half filled with gasoline. One spark, and I would

My 1964 Late Model Modified at Daytona. This car had one of those 427-cubic-inch "mystery" Chevrolet engines under the hood.

have been one of the biggest fires in the county. Fortunately, nothing caught on fire and I got it shut off.

What happened was that I had made a homemade fuel log for my carburetor. It really wasn't very good, and it broke. It sprayed all of the gasoline all over my firewall and inside of my car and had emptied my gas tank.

We then went to Bridge Hampton, Long Island, which was a road race. Turns were basically to the right, and my engine was a wet sump oil system that was designed so the pickup was to the right side of the pan. So every time I made a right turn, I starved the engine for oil.

It only took a few minutes to blow the first engine up in practice. I came into the pits and fixed the engine, with some help, and went out and blew the engine up again. They didn't have a full field of cars, so I got to start the race.

I lasted a few laps, and the engine failed again. By then, I had used up all of my stuff as far as parts and everything I could gather up. We went across the ferry to New England and got a motel there. The next morning on the outskirts of Boston, we went into a Chevrolet dealership.

The young guy behind the counter said they didn't have what I was looking for, a high performance short block engine, but there was a "take out" in the garage. A "take out" was when a customer said they were hearing a noise, or some type of complaint, and the dealership took it out and put in a new one. He said we could have the one on the pile for $50. I went and looked at it, and it had everything I needed.

So I bought it and took off for Oxford, Maine. There was a little Chevy dealership about a half-block from the racetrack. They allowed me to work on my race car there. I did all the work I needed on the car.

I took it to the track and won my first NASCAR Winston Cup Series race. What a thrilling night it was for me, too.

Two nights later, we were at Fonda (New York) Speedway, and I started reasonably close to the front. Well, Tiny Lund and J.T. Putney got into it, and I became the center attraction of the greatest wreck at the speedway in a long time. It really tore the car up bad and squashed it on the right side to the point that it was 39 inches shorter than it was supposed to be—that was a really long way.

The right rear fender was pushed up, adding to the 39-inch deficit we had on that car. I had a cousin who lived in New Jersey, but west of New York City. He was a really neat guy by the name of Dave Demarest. I called him up at midnight on Thursday night. I told him I had wrecked my car pretty bad and that since he worked in a body shop, I needed him to help me fix the car.

I told him we needed to patch the car for Islip, New York, by Saturday night. He told me he would get what body parts we needed, for me to get some rest and to meet him there in the morning. So he rounded up the fender, bumper, hood and some of the other pieces we needed because they were too ruined to even stretch out.

We got down there and worked through the night on Friday and left for Islip with that car and got there about 4:30 p.m. John Bruner, Sr. was the chief steward for NASCAR and traveled with the circuit. I walked up to sign in for my pit passes, and he said, "I just told NASCAR we would never see that thing again." I said, "Well, it's not very pretty, but it is here."

Well, that night I won the second NASCAR Winston Cup Series race of my career. The car looked bad, but ran good.

Here I am being interviewed by Larry Mendelson after winning my second NASCAR race at Islip Speedway in July of 1966.

Robert Harper from Jackson, Mississippi, owned this 1961 Ford Modified. I drove this at Daytona in the Modified race in 1965.

Demo Derby at Bowman-Gray

12

As you know already from the 1979 Daytona 500 story, Bobby didn't back away from too many people in his time. And it seems that attitude started early on his racing career. Sometimes a man has to do what a man has to do. At Bowman-Gray (North Carolina) Stadium, Curtis Turner found out what the wrath of Allison was all about. NASCAR didn't like what happened, but the fans there that night sure as heck loved what they saw.

Winston-Salem, North Carolina, had Bowman-Gray Stadium, which was built around a football field. They just paved around the outside of the playing field and had very little banking, if any, so it was kind of a narrow place. But kind of an interesting place.

So I was in my little Chevelle that I already won a fortune with that year. Curtis Turner was there to drive Junior Johnson's factory Ford. Curtis was a pretty flamboyant character. He was never unfriendly to me, but we weren't friends.

Curtis showed up and he looked like he had been "preparing" for the race—he showed up in a suit and tie with a big smile on his face. He qualified behind me, and when they dropped the green flag, he just drove me straight into the wall in turn one. The track was small enough that I was able to have the collision without much damage to the car, but it cost me a lot of spots on the track. He went on and drove into the lead.

I worked my way back and was determined to do the best I could and win the race, if I could. It took me probably 100 laps to catch him. I decided I was going to do my best to pass him fair and square.

Well, I attempted that again and he just ran into me. I got out of the mess and backed away from him. He'd kept the lead, but I would attempt to pass him again. "Boy, this just isn't right," I thought to myself. In my attempt to pass him, and not backing off, I end up wrecking again.

This time I was really mad about that, because my car was really damaged. The caution came out, and Curtis was the first car behind the pace car and I was over in the middle of the infield with a damaged car and pretty much out of the race. So I got to thinking, "This guy isn't going to do this to me." I just went across the grass and struck him right in the left front fender and wrecked him. Well, whoever was second just pulled out around the mess and followed the pace car.

Curtis Turner put his car into reverse and backed into me. I ran into him, he'd back into me, and I'd back into him. We were out in the infield in the football field just sliding around and banging into each other. The old trick in those days was you put it in reverse so you could take care of your radiator and everything.

Here we were backing around like a couple of Joie Chitwood Thrill Show drivers trying to wreck each other. Finally, we got bent up enough where both of us got stopped out in the middle. NASCAR's chief steward, John Bruner, came running across the infield. By then, the pace car had stopped the field and people were coming over the grandstand wall onto the field—this was an exciting event going on. Bruner came yelling over to me, "Don't ever run into Curtis Turner. Don't ever run into this big-time racer." I said, "Did you notice he ran into me first?" Bruner replied, "Don't tell me, I'm just telling you not to ever run into him again."

Well, all that did was make me a little madder. They ended up having to halt the race—it was a real riot.

13

The "Missing" Victory

When you read various books recording the number of victories for NASCAR, you will notice that some say Bobby has 84 victories and others 85. Bobby will tell you, of course, that the ones listing 85 are correct. NASCAR, however, officially lists Bobby at 84.

Either way, Bobby has the explanation of what happened that night at Bowman-Gray (North Carolina) Stadium and why he wasn't given the victory. Which, incidentally, would give him one more than Darrell Waltrip and alter the record books stating they are tied for third on the all-time wins list. When you're done with what Bobby has to say, you decide if he has 85 wins.

I really liked Bowman-Gray and thought my little Chevelle could really do a good job there. I did win there with that same car a year later and was pretty proud of that.

About three years later, in 1971, we were still running there once a year. By that time, NASCAR was having a tough time getting a full field of cars at the short tracks. So it was a put-down to have an event and not have a full field. NASCAR decided to let the Grand American cars run to fill the field. They had smaller engines and

This is the same car I got that "missing" win with at Bowman-Gray Stadium, for which NASCAR never gave me credit for the victory. Here it is at Daytona for the Paul Revere 25.

tires that couldn't compete with the Grand Nationals.

Anybody who wanted to could run a Grand American car. I was driving for Holman-Moody at the time, and we were having great success on the big tracks with their 1969 Mercury. I also ran a few races with their 1971 Ford Torino.

It was time to go to Bowman-Gray, and Ralph Moody said they weren't going to run their car there because it was tough on equipment. I told them I really wanted to go there, and they said they had Melvin Joseph's Mustang sitting there. He liked me, and I liked Melvin. So I agreed to do that and they said it would run good.

So we took the Mustang, and the car qualified well. Most of the guys thought the little cars couldn't qualify with the little engines. The race started, and pretty soon I was out front. I ended up winning the race. When it was over, a lot of people were pretty annoyed that this Grand American car had won.

There was some hemming and hawing and people talking about, but I just went on my way. For about a year or two, I got credit for the win. Then the results started showing that I hadn't won the race. I let it go at that, thinking they had given the win to Richard Petty.

Richard is everybody's hero, so I assumed they gave it to him. For many years, I just ho-hummed that. During that same period of time, Tiny Lund had won two Grand National races with his Grand American car. One was at North Wilkesboro and the other was at Hickory Speedway. The one at North Wilkesboro was a pretty major event.

But as I looked, the person who finished second to Tiny Lund didn't get credit for the win. I got to wondering about that and thought they gave my win to Richard Petty, and the Pope can't take a win away from Richard Petty. So I'm out of the picture.

Much later, I found out nobody got the win. So it makes me very entitled to that 85th win. I ran the race under the conditions the race was run under in those days, and I won the race. Tiny Lund won the two races he won and should get credit for them.

So that makes me the winner and gives me 85 wins.

This is Melvin Joseph's No. 49 Mustang that I drove to win both the 1971 Busch and Cup races at Talladega. This is also the car I earned that "missing" victory in at Bowman-Gray Stadium.

The Allison gang sitting around the living room in 1969. From left to right: that's Clifford, Davey

14

How Bobby Met Judy

Everyone has a story of how they met their mate. Well, it's not too much of a stretch of the imagination that Bobby met Judy through racing, is it?

Bobby tells of this man, Ralph Stark, who owned a race car and sold spare parts to different racers. Ralph, according to Bobby, took a real liking to this young driver at Hollywood (Florida) Speedway. Well, Ralph just so happened to have a sister-in-law named Judy.

After a race one night, Bobby stole a glance across a restaurant and saw Judy. She, in turn, stole the heart of a champion.

Judy and me sharing a quiet moment in 1979.

After the races, we'd all go to a little drive-in restaurant and have a midnight snack. It really was the normal thing back in those days. So I went there, and I had a friend by the name of Bob Jannelle with me. A lot of people in the racing circles might remember him. He had been a friend since high school.

One of my favorite parts of winning is getting a kiss from Judy in Victory Lane. This smooch came after I won the Trenton 300 in 1972.

He was sitting in the grandstands on this night. We went to this restaurant, and he pointed out this little blonde girl who was with Ralph and Carolyn Stark. Bob says, "That gal over there was really interested in you at the races. You should go say hello to her." Sure enough, I looked over there and there was this real cutie pie. I walked over and said hello, and Carolyn introduced me to her younger sister, saying she had come to live with them and was going to the nearby high school.

So I said, "Well, I'd really like to get acquainted. Why don't you let me drive you home?" and she said, "Okay." Their house was about one and a half blocks from the restaurant. Judy got in the pickup truck with me, and about one and a half hours later, I got her home. It was kind of a long ride for that distance, I guess.

Anyway, we talked and I thought she was really neat and I wanted to see her again. I guess it was about a week later, and the same situation presented itself again and I was able to give her a ride home from the restaurant again.

Judy reminds me that on an occasion right around that time, I needed to see Ralph for some spare parts in the midweek period. She said I showed up to pick up these parts all dressed in nice clothes instead of my work clothes. Thinking about it now, I have to laugh. I did ask if she could go down to the restaurant with me, and she did.

That part worked out okay, and we began to date. We really had a great time together, and a love affair started. We went on and got married, and Davey, Bonnie, Clifford and Carrie came along.

Judy just became *the* number-one racing wife.

This family shot was taken right after I won the Atlanta 500 in 1978. That's our daughter Carrie between Judy and me with (l-r) Davey, Bonnie and Clifford holding the checkered flag.

Judy and me relaxing out back on the gazebo in October of 2002.

One and Dung

Bobby was known for his athletic abilities on the race track, his quick wit with the public, his charming smile and his determination to win. That's why he should never have taken to a ski slope on a family vacation.

He went from champion driver to chump skier in just one trip. Not to mention he got into one heck of a predicament that really stunk.

We were always looking for something outside our environment to do for a break or enjoyment. So several of the family members got together and decided we should go to Colorado and go snow skiing in the winter.

I did some water skiing and could do that reasonably okay. I was always reluctant to do anything in snow and cold weather, but they convinced me that we all should go snow skiing.

So we got one of the condos out there and got all lined up. The next day we had to get a set of skis and get some instruction so we could go up this ski lift to come down the slope. First of all, I didn't pay much attention to any of the instruction. Second of all, there was little instruction anyway.

But I got my skis and headed up the ski lift, and we passed these different markings. There were the green ones, yellow, red and yellow, and then just the red. We were all the way at the top of the lift, and I said I would ride back down.

They told me I couldn't ride back down, I had to ski down. Well, okay, I'll just ski down. They then informed me I was on the expert slope and I had better know how to ski. I told them I would do okay.

I started down the hill and I fell and crashed. I got up and brushed myself off. I started back down the hill and fell, and crashed, and stumbled all over again. I brushed myself off, went another five feet and fell down again. I mean, I was really having a hard time getting down the side of the mountain.

So I saw the Ski Patrol and hollered over to them and told them I needed a ride down the hill. They said I couldn't ride down in their buggy unless I had broken bones. I said, "Hang on, I'll break one of my legs or something." They told me I had to ski downhill.

Goofing off in a Go-Kart at Disney World in 1993. Hey, it sure beats skiing!

Reluctantly, I got back on my skis and started working my way back down the hill. Finally, I got to the point where I could ski for several feet at a time and started feeling really confident in myself. I could see this path that looked like a shortcut to where I wanted to turn the skis in.

Well, I started across this path, and it turned out to be a dike with two pools of the community sewer on either side. I got about halfway across, got tangled up, turned the wrong way, and out into this pool I went. I absolutely was swimming with all these lumps in the water having just one heck of a time.

So that ended my skiing. Those were my two ski trips—my first and my last.

Here I am at Talladega in 1973 teaching Davey how his racing career will start.

Racing with Davey

There wasn't anyone who roared onto the NASCAR Winston Cup Series scene quite like Davey Allison. Following in his father's footsteps, the second-generation racer captured the hearts and following of millions— just like his dad.

Bobby and Davey raced against each other for only two seasons. But when it came to father and son becoming racer vs. racer, Bobby had a unique way of putting it all into perspective.

Davey and me at Desoto (Florida) Speedway in 1986.

My situation with Davey was really good, because when the green flag went down I could treat Davey like any other competitor. You know, I feel like I was able to do that my whole career. I was able to do that with Neil Bonnett and I was able to do that with Red Farmer.

Red was my hero early on, and he won a lot when I first started racing. But when I got to winning, I began to win more than Red Farmer, and I thought that was great. I could take everybody, even when Davey came along, and separate him from the family to a competitor.

I didn't want to do anything wrong, any harm to him or to anyone. But I wanted to be in front of him. So that's how that deal worked.

Bobby Goes Boom at Dega

In 1987, Davey and Bobby were racing each other at Talladega Superspeedway when history was made. Bobby's contribution has affected racing on superspeedways to this day. Davey's part made the record books and memory banks of fans galore.

I was in the Stavola Brothers Racing car—a red and white No. 22 Buick, a beautiful car—and had qualified up front and was fairly pleased with the car. I was running pretty good, but had slipped back a few spots and wasn't really concerned about that.

We were coming through the tri-oval, and I was in a pack of cars and my engine blew up. It blew up so bad that the entire front of the crankshaft came off with all the pulleys and drive equipment on it. It came completely off the motor and went under the car.

I ran over it, which made the car hop into the air. But also, the tire hit the crankshaft and blew out, causing the car to jump into the air. It spun around and made this great big horrible crash with cars going everywhere. I missed the flagstand by about an inch and tore down some of the safety fencing on the front stretch.

This is the section of fencing I took out at Talladega in 1987. Thankfully, nobody was hurt when this happened. I was done for the day, but Davey went on to win his first race.

Davey in the No. 28 car after they went to the all-black design.

I ended up sliding around on the race track, and Phil Parsons slid into me and spun me around a few more times. I had oil all over me because it broke my dry-sump oil tank. It was in my eyes, so that I couldn't see, and all over my face and uniform.

Sitting in the car, stunned, I remember the safety crew coming up to the car, and all I could think was I knew I got into the catch fence. I asked the safety crew how many people were hurt. They told me nobody was hurt, I was the only one.

The rule always was that you had to go to the infield care center. So they rode me around, taking me the long way. I thought, "Yeah, they're taking me this way so I don't have to look at all the bodies on the race track back there where I tore the fencing down."

We got around to the infield hospital, and Dr. Hardwick—one of my very favorite people—was running things at the time. He came out to the ambulance and said, "Okay, shut the helicopters off, we don't need them." Well, if they can shut the helicopters off, then that meant nobody was hurt—which was really good news to me. So he checked me over and asked how I was. I was okay, except for the oil all over me, and he cleaned me up a bit.

He released me and told me to go back to the garage and do whatever I wanted. I told Judy, "C'mon, let's go home." She said that we should stay because Davey was running really good. So I moped a little bit about it and then realized it was a good idea.

We stayed there and watched Davey put on a performance that we all will remember forever. Davey won his first race (of 19), and we got to go to Victory Lane with him. We tore down the fence, and Davey got us to Victory Lane anyway.

It was really a great event for us.

The race and Bobby's crash inspired NASCAR to utilize restrictor plates on NASCAR Winston Cup cars to slow the speeds and make for safer racing. On July 13, 1993, Davey sustained fatal injuries in a helicopter accident at Talladega. His loss affected the sport deeply.

This is Davey and me practicing at Daytona in 1987. This was just before Davey qualified on the outside

18

Battlin' Bobby and Son Clifford

Clifford Allison was Davey's younger brother. He dabbled in racing here and there. He raced Late Models and was a competitor in the NASCAR Busch Series on a part-time basis. Bobby was never known to back down from an on-track confrontation, even more so when it came to standing up for his sons.

While helping Clifford out at one race, Bobby got a little more than he was bargaining for in the battle department. He left with a lasting memory from the race and a souvenir he wasn't counting on taking out of there.

Well, one night at Birmingham (Alabama) Raceway, Clifford was racing and got into some fender-banging with a competitor. Bobby was there that night and ended up more involved than he would have liked to have been. Especially since he had to race at Talladega the next day in his NASCAR Winston Cup ride.

But sometimes, things just don't go the way you plan—or hope.

My son Clifford behind the wheel.

I was really tickled with Clifford's efforts. He would race some weeks, while other weeks he wanted to go ride dirt bikes. That was so different than the way Davey had been—he wanted to be at the race track every time.

So I was pleased to hear Clifford was again interested in racing. He was at Birmingham and running pretty good. Well, one of the other youngsters crashed into him and really tore the car up bad. I went over to the car, and it was all tangled up in the backstretch guard rail.

I said, "Clifford, are you okay?" He said he was okay. "Well, if you're okay, then you had better go over there and tell that boy that ran you into the fence that he needs to straighten up a little bit. He did you wrong two or three times before he completely wrecked you."

He says, "Yeah, Dad, I'll go tell him." So Clifford got out of the car—we were on the backstretch, and all the cars were stopped on the front stretch. He went to the front stretch, and I followed him.

This is one of my son Clifford's first race cars. Notice the bungee cords holding the hood down.

He walked up to this little bitty kid who was in this other car and said, "You wrecked me, and I'm really mad at you about wrecking me." In the meantime, the other guy's mechanic floored me with a punch.

I mean, he really clobbered me. It came as such a complete surprise. I guess I should have been paying a little better attention. I had no idea that somebody was going to swing at me over anything that we did.

Well, I'll tell you what. That swelled my eye up and blackened my face. It looked like I had really been in a terrible brawl. I was kind of concerned, because I was driving the Stavola Brothers car and had to run Talladega the next day.

I won Talladega the next day with my swelled-up eye and bruised up face. I was proud of Clifford, at any rate, and if I had to take a few licks along the way—I guess that's the way it had to be.

Clifford Allison suffered fatal injuries during a NASCAR Busch Series practice at Michigan International Speedway on August 13, 1992. He was 28.

My NASCAR Busch Series car that Clifford—pictured—pretty much built by himself. I won the NASCAR Busch Series race at Daytona in this car in 1988 and Clifford drove it some during that year, too.

19

El Toro! That Darn Matador

Bobby Allison was one of the few drivers who crawled behind the wheel of an AMC Matador on the race track. He owned one of the oddly shaped cars with the red, white and blue paint scheme and also drove one for Roger Penske.

During the 1977 season, Bobby tried like crazy to make the Matador a winning car, both as an owner/driver and as a hired gun. He tells of the trials and tribulations he faced in both capacities.

The Matador was really an unusual deal for me. I was running my own Chevrolets and just struggling along. In 1974, NASCAR changed the rules, going from the 427-cubic-inch engines to a 366-cubic-inch engine. So, we built all 366-cubic-inch equipment.

I was running my own equipment and couldn't buy a dozen of everything. I was having to do one engine at a time and maybe get some kind of spare. I was just really scraping by, and we were doing poorly—and NASCAR changed the rules again and went down to a 358-cubic-inch engine.

The AMC Matador in a familiar position—getting fixed.

The change was better for everybody, but it didn't fit my deal. I really was struggling, and we were at Michigan for the first race there that year. I knew Roger Penske a little bit from running in the IROC cars and had attempted his Indy car for him. But we didn't have a real close relationship or anything.

Roger told me that Gary Bettenhausen just got hurt and he had this Matador that he really had to run. He asked me if I would drive the car at Daytona for the July race. I was in a real predicament with my own stuff, but had to have Coca-Cola on the car.

Roger said we could put Coke on the hood and the Coca-Cola script on the quarter panels, but he had to have AMC on there, too. So I called the folks at Coke, and they were okay with it.

So I went to Reading, Pennsylvania, where their first race shop was located, and looked at the car and set up. I told them that for Daytona, I would like to change the chassis setup, and the car looked good. The car was fast, but it wasn't very reliable.

They said they had this deal with Traco Engines and weren't allowed to do anything to the engines. It had been a bit of a problem, but they knew the car would run and go around the race track good.

So I told them for me to drive the car, we needed to make some changes to the chassis. They said they could do that and set the car up the way I liked. We went to Daytona, and on the first day of qualifying I had the fast time. I was going to be on the pole, it was around 3 p.m., three cars were left to qualify—and it began to rain.

NASCAR decided to let those three cars qualify the next day at 7 a.m. One of those cars was David Pearson. Now, I had been faster than him in practice and was confident that I could be faster under him in pretty similar conditions.

But at 7 a.m. the next morning, it was 40 degrees cooler than it was when we qualified. David Pearson beat me by 1/10,000th of a second—he just barely beat me

The famous Matador blowing up again—this time at the season opener at Riverside in 1977.

out for the pole, putting me in the outside pole.

The race started on Fourth of July, and I went directly into the lead and led the race. I led the race and was just dominating the race. With 15 laps to go, the engine started to miss and the car slowed down, and I was struggling.

They told me over the radio to keep going, it wouldn't blow up, it just slowed down. So I kept going and finished fifth. Well, for me, it was a really good deal because Roger Penske paid me to drive the car. It was the first time in my career I actually got paid a salary to drive the car, along with some of the winnings. I had no equipment expense; all I had was my own living and traveling expenses. So it was a profitable run for me, and they were pretty happy with it.

The next race for that car was Michigan, and Roger told me to run the car again. So I jumped in the car and it was the same thing. We qualified up front, the race got started and I was leading the race. Then, with 15 laps to go, the engine started missing and I slowed down.

So I said, "Roger, why don't we see what's wrong and why this thing keeps missing?" He said, "No, I have a deal with Traco and they said we couldn't look at the engine. And they said Bobby Allison can't even look under the hood. We'll have our guy be there with the engine, we're building the engines and we'll do it our way."

I just thought we should look at the engine because it did the same thing every race. I wanted to look and see why it did that. Roger said no, that Traco did the engines and for me to stay away from everything.

So we went to the next race and the same thing started to happen. I was leading the race, the engine started to miss, and I lost the race. We then went to the Southern 500 (Darlington) and I was leading the race and the engine started to miss; I lost the race.

This happened several times. Finally we were going to Ontario (California) Speedway for the final race of the year.

Here I am wrenching on the AMC Matador in 1977.

74

This car (to the right) marks the shortest term of employment I ever had in a race car. It's a Shadow with a 427-cubic-inch Chevy-powered, fuel-injected engine, shown here at Riverside in 1972. The car competed in the Can-Am Challenge Cup Series. I did a few laps and was promptly fired because I went faster than the regular driver.

Here I am putting a Porsche through the ringer at Riverside in 1973. This was the first year of the IROC Series; we switched to a Camaro for the next year.

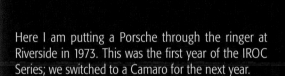

This Datsun was owned by Peter Brock. I drove this car at Laguna Seca and Riverside Speedways in 1972.

20

Hey, Where's My Patient?

The saying is you can't keep a good man down. And with Bobby, you couldn't keep a good racer away from the track—even if it meant being his own doctor.

The week before Ontario was an open week, so they decided to have an IROC (International Race of Champions) event at Riverside (road course). This was the second year of IROC (1985), and we were running the Camaro. So the IROC race got going and a guy got into me, and I got into the concrete part of the guard rail and crashed really hard.

They hauled me off to the hospital. I was lying there with my hospital gown on. My uniform was gone, my underwear was gone, and all I had on was this one-sided hospital gown as I lay on this emergency room cot. And the doctor didn't come in. They X-rayed me and stuck me back in there and left me there. I kept waiting.

After quite a while, maybe a couple of hours, some friends of mine from Bessemer, Alabama, showed up. Tom Gloor and T.D. Hawton had flown out there in T.D.'s plane to see the race and knew I had gotten hurt. So they came to the hospital to see how I was doing.

Tom Gloor always referred to me as "Stroker." In those days, a "stroker" was someone who always did well and got accused of doing it with an illegal engine, which was a "stroker" engine. But I never did that.

So he came into the emergency room where I was lying and said, "Stroker, how are you?" I told him, "Boy, I really hurt, but I'm mad because I haven't seen anybody in a couple hours. If I could find my clothes, I'd leave."

He told me my clothes were right outside the door in a cart. I told him to get them for me. He got me my clothes; I put them on and I went to the hotel. I was lying in bed there and the phone rang—it was the track doctor, who also had been at the hospital.

He said, "Where are you?" I said, "Where did you call?" He said, "Well, you get back to this hospital. I didn't release you." I told him, "Doc, you had me—and you lost me. I'm not coming back."

The doctor went on to tell me I could be hurt really bad. I told him to give me the name of the injury and I would call my doctor back home. He told me my sixth vertebra had a vertical fracture, top to bottom. He told me that everything was in place and everything would be okay if I didn't hurt it again.

I called Dr. Springer back at home and he told me to do whatever I wanted to do, as long as I could put up with whatever pain I had. So I told him I was going to run the race the next day.

I won the race on Sunday, and the broken back probably helped me. I was known to run off the track at Riverside, and on that Sunday I was careful to stay on the smooth part because it didn't hurt as bad when I hit the bumps. But I won the race.

While I was leading at Rockingham in 1976, a lapped car made contact with my Roger Penske-owned car on a restart and—as you can see—I ended up rolling over several times. I broke some ribs, and my eye was cut so bad that both my eyes had to be bandaged shut for three days.

AP/WWP

21

Finally a Win, but Fined By a Tail

Bobby Allison drove for Roger Penske in 1975 and prospered, only to finish a few positions shy of that elusive win. Bobby had worked on his own Matador and struggled. After so many close runs and runner-up finishes with the Matador in 1977, he finally tasted the sweetness of victory.

Finally, at Ontario Speedway, Bobby bulled the Matador to a win. But it seems NASCAR was a little bullish about his win, too. And the resulting penalty wasn't that sweet at all. Matter of fact, it kind of stung.

After I won at Riverside with the fractured vertebra, I went to Traco to their engine shop to see what was wrong with these Matador engines. I walked into their shop, and they weren't too happy to see me. I looked at this engine they were disassembling, and it had a broken rocker arm.

But the rocker arm was an aftermarket, a little cheap aluminum piece that you could buy in the neighborhood speed shop. Nothing high-performance about it, and it happened to be a part I recognized that had a very bad reputation.

I said to this guy, Jim Travers—whose nickname, of all things, is Crabby—"Crabby, nobody can run those kind of rocker arms. They break on anything!" He said, "We bought a case of those things, and we're going to use them until they are used up."

I told him we were done with them and we were now going to use Norris stainless steel rocker arms in this thing, which had been a good reliable thing for the Chevys.

Norris was close by, so I ran over to Norris and picked up a set of rocker arms.

We cleaned the engine up, polished it up a little bit, and we were careful putting the thing back together again. But we didn't do anything really special. We put the engine back together and headed out to Ontario.

This is my No. 12 AMC Matador that I ran in Winston Cup races in 1977.

The engine did not start missing when I was leading late in the race. And I won the race—my first win in the Matador. We were really happy about that. We went to the press box and had a big ol' time with all the reporters up there.

That one, I didn't fly my Aerostar to Ontario for that particular race. I had an airline ticket and went to the Los Angeles Airport and took the all-nighter to Atlanta. I got off the airplane in Atlanta at 7 a.m., and the *Atlanta Journal-Constitution* was sitting there in a rack.

The headline read "Allison fined $9,100."

My mouth fell down, I put my money in the machine and got a paper out. It said, "In the postrace inspection, NASCAR had discovered illegal roller tappets." I felt pretty bad about that. I had found out that they had roller tappets in the engine when we had it apart at Traco.

But I really felt I wasn't that concerned about it because I had seen roller tappets in another competitor's engine. And they were at a point where everybody could see when they took the intake manifold off, it had roller tappets and NASCAR okayed it. I felt if that guy could run them, then it should be okay for me, too, and shrugged it off.

Well, I got to Atlanta the next day and found out we'd been fined $9,100. We had never heard of a fine anything like that kind of money. That $9,100 took almost all of the winnings ($15,125) . It was a 500-mile race, but in those days some of the races didn't pay too well.

I got a little information on that that has turned into kind of a cute story, too. I asked a friend of mine, who was riding in the NASCAR plane at the time, "What happened?"

He said, "I gotta tell you, we were walking out to the plane and Bill France, Jr. was really mad because you won a race with that stinking Matador. Then, it's caught with an illegal part. Walking out to the airplane, he looks up at his airplane and sees the tail." The number on the NASCAR plane was 9100N.

He looked at the plane and said, "9100, 9100, that's what I'm gonna fine the son of a gun, $9100." So that's where the fine came from for that race.

This is an AMC Hornet I drove in 1976 near our shop in Hueytown.

Here I am standing with my fleet—a GMC pickup, my favorite Superstar Aerostar airplane, and my No. 12 Buick—in 1988 at the airport in Daytona. My son Clifford pretty much built that car by himself. I drove it to victory in the Daytona Busch race that year. Notice how everything has the same paint scheme.

22

Who Went 200 mph First?

On March 24, 1970 at Talladega Superspeedway, Buddy Baker was given credit for "officially" breaking the 200-mph barrier on a closed course. The large tri-oval with 33-degree banked turns of Talladega was the perfect setting to break the mark, too.

Driving a winged Dodge-Chrysler, Baker was the only driver there that day. But according to some other sources, the mark may have been set a week earlier—just not as "officially" as everyone might think.

The Mario Rossi-owned No. 22 Dodge Daytona. This was taken in 1970 at Daytona. See how small the frontstretch grandstands were back then?

We went to Talladega with a one-winged Dodge with that blue No. 88 on it. All the Chrysler drivers went there on Tuesday and all the Chrysler drivers got to drive that car—but me. The chief engineer, Larry Rathgeb, and his chief assistant, George Wallace, were there.

The chief engineer had a little resistance to my constant request to adjust my car to whatever I wanted rather than drive it by the book. Chrysler's book said "this was the best way for this car to run the fastest and you'll win the race" if you did it their way.

I never believed that.

Anyway, he wasn't very fond of me, and that was probably the biggest contribution to that

Me and the crew after winning the Atlanta 500 with the winged Dodge Daytona in 1970.

particular feeling of the engineer toward me. The public relations guy, Frank Wylie, was a big fan of Buddy Baker and big fan of Charlie Glotzbach. He really didn't care too much for me, because I was really known to go run my Chevrolets somewhere on a day they didn't want to run their Dodge. I wanted to be running if there was something running.

Tuesday went by and everybody got to run this car—but me. They were running about 196 mph. Richard Petty, Pete Hamilton, Charlie, Buddy, Richard Brickhouse, James Hylton and whoever else had a Dodge at the time.

So we went back Wednesday. Everybody got to run this car again—but me. They basically told me to stay off to the side and to shut up because I would get my turn. We went back Thursday and everybody got to run this car—but me.

We went back Friday, and the same thing happened. Now they are up to about 197 mph. We went back Saturday, and it was about 3 p.m. and they were finally right at the high 197-mph range, but not 198. They said, "Okay, Allison, you can run."

So I got out and I went 199.6 mph 199.7 mph, then 199.9 as my best lap. But it didn't reach 200 mph. They were pretty impressed and knew they had to come back again to figure the deal out of how I went so much faster than the other guys. We couldn't run on Sunday until after lunch because of the church laws.

They wanted to know how "this jerk from Alabama could be almost three mph faster than our fastest, best guys?" I was faster than Buddy and Charlie. They couldn't figure how I was doing it. So we got back there on Sunday, and George Wallace, who had the car instrumented pretty well, gathered all the guys around.

"Come here, I'll show you all how Allison beat you," he said. He had this tape of the steering wheel movement matched to the contour of the track. He showed how everyone drove the car slightly moving their hands back and forth on the wheel.

I kept my hands steady on the wheel.

The other way scrubbed speed off, so that's why I was faster. George told the other guys to start holding the steering wheel straight to see how they would do. Buddy went 199, Charlie went 199, and so did the other two guys who were there.

Finally, it got to be about 4 p.m. and they said, "Okay Allison, you can take another lap." So I got in the car and I went out there. As I came by where they were, I saw 200.001 mph on the electric clock. They were using the same clock for everybody.

Next lap, I went 200.009 mph, right at 201, and the engine blew up. It blew oil out all over the windshield; I mean, this was a major disaster. And I had to save this car by looking out the right window at the wall and guiding that car that's sliding in oil. But I didn't crash.

They came out there and got the car. They said they had to have a meeting. The test was definitely over. Everybody was sworn to secrecy, because we didn't want Ford to know we ran 200 mph. So everyone was sworn to secrecy, and if anyone let it out that we ran 200 mph, they would have been fired.

I went home with my lips sealed. Dodge announced they were going to make a speed run with Buddy Baker to go 200 mph. So they took the same car with the same clocks, and Buddy Baker went 200 mph.

This is Bobby Isaacs (No. 71) and me (No. 22) in our famed Dodge Daytona winged cars going three wide with James Hylton (No. 48) at Talladega in 1969.

Now, he never went 200.009, he went 200.001 mph. But he did make 200 mph. All Buddy says is that he made the first "official" run.

23 Richard, Cale, David and Dale

Even though the great competitors of the early era of NASCAR were notorious for some of their intense battles, there was still a level of respect for each other. Richard Petty and Bobby sold a lot of tickets to races so fans could watch them go fender to fender and battle for a win.

The rivalry got so big that NASCAR had to call the two in for a little talk. They talked, the drivers listened and went right back out onto the track to do battle again. Bobby is very honest about his feelings for racing with Richard and how competitive Cale Yarborough was back in the day. Bobby also did battle with David Pearson, second on the all-time wins list, and that upstart driver during their time, Dale Earnhardt.

Richard Petty was the all-time competitor. He raced everywhere and he ran really, really well on dirt. I didn't know too many guys who did well on dirt and pavement. Red Farmer was the best of all of those that I knew.

I won on pavement easily, but I struggled on dirt. I finally won a few times on dirt, but it was really difficult and different from the normal routine I would use to win a race on pavement. Richard Petty would win on the big tracks, the little tracks, the dirt tracks, and he dominated his part of the sport.

He came with the most and best equipment—the most tires, the most help and all those things. But he really did the job and established a goal to shoot at. See, the other guys like David Pearson were also good on dirt, but David didn't go to every race. Cale Yarborough was the same way. Cale went to a lot of races, but then didn't go to a lot of races. Richard Petty was always there.

It became a deal where a lot of times it would be me racing Richard Petty, Richard Petty racing me. Sometimes, we both wanted the same piece of race track. And sometimes we argued a little about who was entitled to that particular part of the race track. But all that did was excite the fans.

We'd race each other, we'd bend each other's fenders some, but we always made it back to the finish line. You know, in later racing, a lot of times guys would get into a competitive tussle and somebody would not end up making it to the finish line. That was unfortunate, but that was a fairly common occurrence in racing.

I was really proud that Richard and I could bump and bang and still not tear the cars up to the point we couldn't keep going. Of course, a few times I'm sure he thought it was my fault. I always knew it was always all his fault.

That attitude probably kept me encouraged to go on to the next event. You know, sometimes when you've done poorly, at least if you think you've done right, it helps your attitude to be encouraged to go on to the next event.

I have to say that Richard Petty still kept himself classy. He didn't like me and said some things from time to time that let people know he was plenty mad about the way I carried on or a dent I had put in his car.

Richard Petty—cigar and all—takes a break at Pocono in 1974.

AP/WWP

Here Dale Earnhardt "helps" me put on a hat in 1981.

He did things that annoyed me, but at the same time, he was very careful not to embarrass himself and not to alienate any of the fans. The guy deserves so much credit for that. Some days I can feel real good toward him, and sometimes I can be a little bit annoyed that he won a race or two that I thought maybe I should have.

The guy really is The King and deserves all the credit they gave to him.

Cale Yarborough was a really tough nut. He drove hard in every race, and if Cale was 20 laps behind, he was still in there driving hard and racing somebody down to the wire.

One time at Darlington, I was leading the race and Cale was some laps behind and crashed me on the last lap. Lee Roy Yarbrough won the race, and I sat there in the wall all tore up. Cale felt very justified because he had a chance to pass me there on the last lap. He felt very justified with the idea he would attempt to pass me, to show the world he could pass me.

It was just too bad that I didn't make it back around the race track.

David Pearson, on the other hand, was very different. David Pearson could have a really good car, and he'd be sitting back there in fifth, sixth or eighth and not racing anybody. But David Pearson was always famous for taking care of the car, and at the end, he'd be in front of you instead of behind you.

He didn't mingle with me and a few of the other guys. I'm sure there were a couple of guys he was friends with off the track. Living in Spartanburg, South Carolina, he

Cale Yarborough and me—all smiles and enjoying a Coke in 1973.

David Pearson and me talking before a race in 1972.

was near where some of the other guys lived. I lived in Alabama, and so I was out of the immediate circuit anyway. I didn't have a friendship where I spent time with David away from the race track.

Week after week, he'd be sitting back there and I'd think to myself, "Boy, I got him beat today!" And by and by, the checkered flag would come out and there would be David Pearson over there in Victory Lane with them good-looking beauty queens. And there I would be, with my fenders rattling and the old car smoking in second or third.

I'd say, "Boy, I'm really going to have to figure out how to do this. Next week, I'm going to take care of my car and *I'll* be the one to be over there in Victory Lane." It took me a long, long time to really get that accomplished. I made it to Victory Lane a lot of times, but not by taking care of the car.

David Pearson was so good at just really taking care of his car and having it there when he needed it at the end.

Dale Earnhardt came into the picture way late compared to our careers. It was the late 1970s when he showed up. He'd been running the short tracks and running the Sportsman stuff.

I knew Dale, he was a good competitor on the short tracks. But he hadn't done an amazing amount of racing. He was one of those guys who went out there and put on a good show and came home with a win once in a while.

He came into the NASCAR Winston Cup Series and got involved with a fellow from California by the name of Rod Osterlund who had put together a race team. He had enough financial backing to have good equipment, and so forth. Dale came on the scene with a real strong effort.

He won Rookie of the Year (1979) and came back the next year and won the championship. His driving style and his care of the equipment probably contributed to Rod Osterlund's early demise from NASCAR Winston Cup Series racing. I get a good laugh thinking about it. After the second year, Rod decided this was costing him more than he wanted.

From there, Dale went to Richard Childress and then with Bud Moore and stayed with him for a year. Of course, Bud was one of my heroes when I had been with him. Bud's cars, at that time, weren't really the front-runners that they had been and, I felt, could be. Still, Dale Earnhardt did okay with Bud for that season. Then he got together with Richard Childress.

Richard Childress had retired from driving and put the team together. He and Dale formed that partnership that took them on to all those other championships. What a job they did.

This was after Dale Earnhardt won his first championship in 1980 at Riverside with Rod Osterlund as the owner.

AP/WWP

This is Darrell Waltrip, Richard Petty, Cale Yarborough, Buddy Baker, me and David Pearson attempting to sing for the album, "NASCAR Goes Country." Needless to say, it wasn't a real chart burner in 1975.

24 Cotton Owens— Fired Over Tires

Bobby drove for 14 different teams during his illustrious career. He was also an owner/driver off and on for many years. The one good thing about driving for yourself is you're the only one who can fire you. The bad part about driving for yourself is that you pay for everything.

Driving for someone else wasn't as costly, in most cases. But you could get fired as quickly as you got hired, no matter how many races you'd won.

Unfortunately, Bobby experienced the entire gamut. Here, he talks about driving for some of those owners, in chronological order, and what each one was like and what he went through.

Early on, I drove my own car. At the end of the first year when I won a few times with my little Chevelle, I got a chance to go drive for Bud Moore. At the time, Bud Moore had the 1967 Mercurys that were the uni-body car with the constructed frame on them. They were similar to the Fairlanes that Holman-Moody was using, but it was Bud's own construction, ideas and so forth.

The cars were pretty good. But Bud didn't have the backing to run the full schedule. I was in a situation where I was going back to Birmingham to run the Late Models and Modifieds and Montgomery on the weekends. I would just wait for the next time we had a chance to run the Grand Nationals with Bud Moore.

Cotton Owens called me up and told me that David Pearson had just quit. He wanted me to come drive his Dodge. I told him I was driving for Bud Moore. He told me to call Bud and that he'd tell me to come drive for Cotton.

Sure enough, I called Bud and he said he couldn't run much. Cotton said if I'd run his car, he could go to all the races and that Bud couldn't do that. So I went to go drive for Cotton. I thought that was fine.

This is one of those cars owned by Cotton Owens that I got to rebuild. Here we are at Richmond in 1967. That's Dick Johnson (No. 18) to my outside.

So I went over to Cotton's and got into a deal that was really difficult. The cars had become outdated. The rules had been tweaked and tweaked and the chassis had been tweaked by the other people and Cotton had just not kept up.

I said, "Cotton, we need to trim these cars up a little bit and re-do these frames and suspensions a little bit to get them going good." Cotton said to me, "You can do anything you want to do, but any money you spend is your money. Anybody you hire, you have to pay."

I said "Okay, I'll do that." The engines were really good and Cotton had a nice organization with a few employees who were pretty neat guys. At the time, I had at least a strong admiration for Cotton, anyway.

So I called my brother Eddie, and we went to Spartanburg and got a room at the Pine Street Motel. We spent a week rebuilding the first car. We took it to the race track and boy, did it go good. But I didn't win. Still, I was pretty happy.

I told Cotton, "Wow, I'm really, really happy." He says, "Well, David Pearson would have won this race." I was like, "What? Wait a minute, David Pearson is gone."

"Well, that's the way I see it," was his response. I told him next week we'd do really good. And then Cotton informed me we were going to run car No. 2 of the ones in his stable. He told me I could rebuild that one, or run it like it was.

So Eddie and I rebuilt car No. 2 and took that to the race. We ran really good but didn't win the race. I told Cotton, "Well, we'll get a little bit of rest this week and we'll really get 'em next week with this car." He said, "Well, next week we're going to run car No. 3, and you can rebuild it or run it like it is."

So we rebuilt car No. 3 and it really ran good, but didn't win. And I thought I was doing a great job for Cotton and thought I had done a great job of reconstructing his equipment. Finally, we ended up at Birmingham the week before the Fourth of July race at Daytona. Birmingham is my home track, and I felt really good about that.

In those days, you'd get to the track at 10 a.m. and unload, run a lap or two if you wanted, and then at 7 p.m. it was race time. All afternoon, you could run laps and do what you wanted to do. So I was running pretty good. There were a couple of other guys like Richard Petty who were there and running pretty good, too.

I looked at the tires—we were on Firestones then—and we were on a new tire that Firestone had come out with, but wasn't a very good tire for Birmingham. But there happened to be a very good Firestone that was good for Birmingham called a 103. I happened to have 10 103s in my shop in Hueytown. So I got Chuck Looney to run to the shop and bring those tires back.

Chuck came back with the tires; I mounted four and went back out. I was so fast that nobody was even going to be able to race me. I had this race won, and it was about 2 p.m. "They might as well give me the check right now," I thought to myself.

Well, I was standing there leaning on the car, grinning, and the Firestone factory

rep walked over and says, "Jack this car up and take these tires off and give me these 10 tires. I'm putting them on Richard Petty's car. That way, when he wins tonight he'll be on our tires instead of those dang Goodyears."

I said, "Whoa, whoa, whoa wait a minute. They're mine, I brought them from home." He said, "We did not give them to you, we lent them to you—get 'em off." So Cotton was standing there and said, "Give 'em the tires." I told Cotton that wasn't right, and Cotton told me to give them the tires.

This was the second version of my self-owned 1965 Chevelle, shown here in 1967. Every time I got fired or quit a team, I would drive this car to keep racing.

So they rolled my 10 tires away. Now I was mad. I was standing there fuming, and the Goodyear rep walked up, Chuck Blanchard, and said, "Bobby, if you run Goodyear tonight, I'll give you everything you need for free." Well now, I was used to getting one or two free tires for an event. But to get everything we needed for a night, for free, was a big deal for me.

So I told Cotton that we needed to put those Goodyear tires on the car. He said, "Nah, I don't ever run those things." I told Cotton that Firestone had really done us wrong and that we should put Goodyear on the car. He said, "You do whatever you want to do; I'm leaving." And he got in his car and he left. I was there and said to mount the Goodyear tires.

I won the race—and my Firestones finished second right behind me. But I got fired.

25 Holman Turned Out to Be Moody

I ran my own car for the rest of the year. Then Ralph Moody called me and simply said, "You're going to get a phone call in a few minutes and the answer is going to be 'yes,'" and hung up. Several minutes later, Fred Lorenzen called me in and said that Ford had given him a car for Rockingham and I should drive it. I did and ended up winning my first 500-mile race in that car. We ran four times, and I won three times and finished second the other time after crashing right at the end of the race.

But I ended up getting fired by John Holman of Holman-Moody Racing. I drove for Bondy Long, then for Bill Ellis, then for Mario Rossi, and then I was back in my own equipment.

I was really struggling along, and in 1971, Ralph Moody said to me, "Why don't you park that box of yours and come drive my car again." So I got back in the Holman-Moody car and won nine out of 19 starts. It was an incredible, great time for me and just a super deal.

Then John Holman fired me again. The first time I just accepted it. But that time I went to John Holman and said, "John, what have I done wrong?" He said, "You're Ralph Moody's friend—and I hate Ralph Moody."

Here they were partners in one of the most productive operations that had ever come along, and they were known everywhere for their performance for racing. Here John Holman says to me that because I'm Ralph Moody's friend, that I was fired.

Left to right: Pete Benoit from Permatex, me, Ralph Moody and Bill France, Sr. after I took first at Talladega in 1971.

Ironically, I was staying at Moody's house in a spare bedroom that they let me use when I'd come in. I was over there and just about in tears.

Hey Junior, "Kiss My Ass"

hile I was at Ralph's house, the phone rang, and it was Junior Johnson. He told me to meet him over at Richard Howard Furniture Shop in Denver, North Carolina, and that he wanted to talk to me about driving his car. At the time, Richard Howard was the owner of the car and Junior was the operator of the team.

So I went up there and met them. We really had a great performance, but we had a situation where Junior wanted me to communicate through the chain of command. His link to me was his chief mechanic, Herb Naab.

Herb was a neat guy, a very hard worker and a fun guy. I would say, "Junior, why don't we try a 583 gear?" And Junior would act like I hadn't said anything. Or he'd walk up to Herb, and I'd be standing right there, and he'd say, "Tell Bobby we're going to run a 583 gear." I said, "Junior, you can tell me." But he had decided that he wanted to work his team through the chain of command, and it really frustrated me.

If somebody would have come along and included me in a little bit, I probably could have done a better job of handling all that deal. But it was just really a tough deal. Here we were, winning some races and looking pretty good, and this man wouldn't talk to me. So it was about August, and we were there on some short track. Junior walked up and said, "Herb, tell Bobby we're gonna run a 583 gear."

And I said, "Herb, tell Junior to kiss my ass."

Junior Johnson (center), crew chief Herb Naab (right), and me are shown here communicating through the chain of command in 1972.

Well, it stopped Junior from walking up and telling Herb to tell me something, but Junior still never spoke to me. We could go out to eat and we could talk about fishing, coon hunting, or '49 Fords or whatever you wanted to talk about. But he'd never talk about racing to me.

So as the season wound down, Ralph Moody called me and said he thought he had gotten things back together for the next year and wanted to know if I would come back. So I told Junior that I was leaving. Then Ralph didn't end up getting his stuff back together, and I ended up doing my own car again.

27

Bud Is a Bud Again

There I was, really struggling along with that Chevelle, and that's when that Penske deal came along with the Matador. I ran that Matador for two years in 1974 and 1975. I won at Ontario with it at the end of 1974. I won the Darlington Rebel 400 race, the Southern 500 and at Riverside in 1975, too. At the end of 1975, Roger Penske wanted to redesign the nose of the Matador a little

Bud Moore and me standing in front of his No. 15 Ford in 1978.

Here we are doing a pit stop in the Bud Moore-owned No. 15 Ford.

bit to get a little more aerodynamic. The chief designer at AMC refused to consider it, so Roger said they were out of there and he decided to run Mercurys.

In 1976, the Mercury was just really an effort. The team didn't come together, and the car wouldn't go good enough. The Wood Brothers could win with it, but we couldn't. We had a really horrible year with no wins. So I left Penske at the end of 1976.

In 1977, I raced the Matador out of my own shop as the car owner. It was just really a tough deal. We got really good a few times, but didn't get that win. At the end of that season, things were going really tough for me when Bud Moore called me.

He wanted me to drive his Thunderbird. I went to drive for him, and it really was a great year for me. We started 1978 by winning the Daytona 500. We won five times that year. The following year, we had the big deal at Daytona when Cale went to beating on my fist with his nose after that wreck at the end of the race.

I won five times again in 1979, but didn't win the championship either year. I drove for Bud Moore again in 1980 and won four times that year. In fact, I was leading the last-ever Ontario 500 and had a flat tire as I came to pit road and couldn't turn down there right at the end of the race.

Here I am racing Dick May (No. 57) in the No. 15 Thunderbird owned by Bud Moore.

Sixty cars started at Talladega in 1973 and 21 were involved in a wreck on the backstretch. As you can see, I was one of them. Here's what's left of my car. I wasn't hurt, but it sure did hurt that I owned this Chevelle and had to repair it myself.

28

From Championship to Tribulation and Back Again

I left Bud Moore and went with (Harry) Ranier Racing. With him, we raced pretty good. But we really couldn't come together as a team and couldn't work together good enough. The chief mechanic and me couldn't really agree on some of the things we really needed to agree on. So I left there and went to DiGard Racing.

At DiGard, Gary Nelson (crew chief) and Robert Yates (engine builder) were the greatest support crew I had ever had from that standpoint. I really liked the way Gary approached the car, the event and how to do things, and how he ran the radios. He helped me get over being too excited about something that happened on the race track. He also helped me weigh out an adjustment for the car. He had a great effect on me like that.

Robert Yates was a guy who worked for Junior Johnson when I drove for him. I just really admired him, liked him personally and just admired his talent. So the deal was good for me—from that standpoint.

This was taken in 1981 at Riverside as I was sitting in this Harry Ranier-owned Monte Carlo.

Now, the car owner, Bill Gardner, was a whole 'nother story.

We won the Daytona 500 in 1982, and Bill called me up and said, "I want you to do me a favor." I said, "What's that?" He said, "I want you to let me keep the money for the time being, and I'll pay you. But for the time being, let me use the money to pay some bills and do some things because I'm trying to get you a better race team. Just let me have some credit for a short time."

So I said okay. That was in February. By the Fourth of July, I still had not gotten a paycheck from Bill Gardner. And today, he still owes me a lot of money. But it wasn't part of the effort with Robert Yates and Gary Nelson. We raced hard.

The first year together, we did not win the championship.

Victory Lane after winning the Firecracker 400 in 1982. From left to right: my crew chief Gary Nelson, me, engine builder Robert Yates, and owner Bill Gardner.

But during1983—the second year—we got together with Miller High Life for a sponsor, had a really good season again and won the championship.

Bill Gardner decided that the written contract we had was something that he didn't want to honor. It said there would be no second car, and he decided he wanted to have a second car. But he still hadn't paid me the money he owed me. So I decided that I didn't want to sponsor his second car.

That led to friction through the year. We made it through that year, but in 1985, things were even more difficult than the year before. On the Fourth of July that year, at Daytona, I left DiGard Racing and went back on my own.

From there, I went to Stavola Bros. Racing. They were one of the really good outfits I was with in terms of how the team ownership treated me, my family and the racing effort. I really was proud of them and felt like I had a really good deal.

Pretty early on, we won some races, but only a few. But then we won the 1988 Daytona 500 and dominated the entire weekend. We won the 125-mile qualifier on Thursday and the 500 on Sunday, and I thought that was really special, considering I was doing this at age 50.

Now, I don't have any memory of the racing in 1988. But I know what went on and I know what went into the preparation. So I felt good about that part of it. As the season went on, I was not able to win again, and then I got hurt at Pocono. That injury took away so much memory that for everything about that, I have to go to the book and see what really happened.

As for my career, when I go to bragging about something, I won 85 NASCAR Winston Cup races, in nine different brands of cars for 14 different race teams. On one hand, that's quite the accomplishment. Nobody has won in that many brands of cars, and nobody has won for that many different car owners/race teams.

On the other hand, I had a hard time keeping a job—didn't I?

The Daytona 500 Wins

Winning the Daytona 500 is a lifelong dream for anyone who ever strapped themselves into a race car. Children pretend they win it every summer on a playground. Local racers tackle their track every weekend as if they were running the 500. And each February, NASCAR drivers head to Daytona with the hopes of being a winner on the historic 2.5-mile track.

Darrell Waltrip won three championships, but only one Daytona 500. Richard Petty, on the other hand, won seven 500s and the same number of championships. Dale Earnhardt won the same number of championships as Richard, but only one Daytona 500.

Bobby Allison won three Daytona 500 races. The last one was at the age of 50, and it would turn out to be his final trip ever to Victory Lane. If you're going to go out big, it might as well be in the Great American Race.

The Daytona 500 wins were really neat. The first one in 1978 was with Bud Moore. To get to the Daytona 500 that day was a big deal. We wrecked the car on Friday. It had rained on Thursday for the 125-mile qualifiers, so we had to run them on Friday morning instead. On the last lap of that, Buddy Baker slid into me, and I got the bad end of the deal. He got out of the deal with very little damage, but my car got torn up pretty bad.

I was also feeling sick at the time. I started getting this constant nausea, and we didn't know what was wrong. They had talked about a hiatal hernia and all these other things. Really, what it ended up being was a case of bad nerves—work nerves, not racing nerves. It was a reaction from the bad business things I had done, the poor business decisions.

At any rate, here we were on Friday wrecked, and Saturday I laid around feeling sorry for myself and decided I was going to quit. I was going to tell Bud Moore "I quit" and go home. I went down to the garage where the race car was, and the guys had repaired the car and painted it, and lettered it, and it was sitting there looking like a jillion dollars.

Judy and I hoist the trophy after my first Daytona 500 victory in 1978.

I decided if those guys were going to work this hard for me, I couldn't let them down and would give it one more try. I started 33rd and got my first Daytona 500 win— what a thrill.

Bumper, What Bumper?

In 1982, I was driving for DiGard and we had the Buick. The car was a pretty good car. You know, we were pretty strong in practice and it ran decent in the qualifier. But I always had a little bit of a personal problem with Joe Gazaway, or should I say Joe Gazaway had a personal problem with me.

So it was time for Happy Hour on Saturday afternoon. I had not run the NASCAR Busch Series race that afternoon, which was one of the few times I had missed running the Saturday race. But we were there with the car and things were going pretty good.

My crew deserved a champagne bath after helping me win the 1982 Daytona 500.

Here I am winning the Firecracker 400 at Daytona in 1982. That was the year I swept by winning the Daytona 500, too.

Joe walked up and said, "You guys have got to move your back bumper one quarter of an inch before I let you on the race track." I said, "Whoa, wait a minute. We've been through inspection, we've run the Busch Clash and the 125 and now you're telling us we have to move the back bumper?" He said we had to move the back bumper or we couldn't go on the track to practice.

Well, we had to cut the back bumper off the car and we missed the last practice. We never got it done in time to get back on the race track. But we had a little 110 V-wire welder, and we stuck the back bumper on there. We put some pop rivets on the middle plates and we thought that was okay.

The race started on Sunday, and the car was really good. Cale Yarborough got into me in turn four, just racing hard like he normally would do, anyway. But when he did, his front bumper hooked my rear bumper. When he tried to turn away from me, it pulled my bumper off and caused a little bit of a skirmish there and a few cars got the bad end of the deal.

I went on with no back bumper and won the race. Of course, a lot of people said the car was faster with no back bumper. The car was actually faster *with* the back bumper, but it was still fast enough without it and we won the race.

The Final Victory Lap

In 1988, I was driving for Stavola Brothers and we had this new '88 Buick Regal Coupe that Buick had come out with for the year. I was pretty proud of it because Buick had let me go into the clay room the year before and tweak a little bit with the final configuration with the car. I thought that was pretty neat.

I got them to raise the deck lid a little more so we'd have more down force with the standard configuration with the car without having to go with an additional rear spoiler. And I got them to smooth the body work on the front a little bit so it would be nice and slick going through the air. I thought that was pretty good.

This is the No. 12 Miller High Life Buick that I won the Twin 125 and Daytona 500 with in 1988. That sure was a good-looking car.

We got down to Daytona for practice, and my car was really good and I was happy with that. Then the race went on and everybody knows I won the race. But I still don't remember winning the race.

But I have to say at least I knew of the preparation and was confident the car could do really good. Because everything about the car—the effort by the Stavola group (Billy and Mickey Stavola), Keith Almond the engine builder and Jimmy Fennig the crew chief on the car and all my guys—was just a great effort.

I got my third Daytona 500 win.

A crowning achievement. This is me with my No. 22 car and the 1983 NASCAR Winston Cup Series championship trophy outside the Waldorf Astoria in New York City. What a great night this was.

Finally—A Sweet Championship

*T*he championship was something I had worked so hard for, for so many years. I was second so many times.

We'd run good and have something happen late in the season. My first year with Bud Moore in 1978, we won early in the year starting with the Daytona 500. We won five times; we were competitive just about every place we went. But we had a couple of engine failures. Those engine failures would take you so far out of the picture that the point loss would be too great to overcome.

So I had been second in points several times, and finally, in 1983, we were able to get the win. But even that didn't come easy.

This is one of my favorite pictures of all time. That's my dad, Edmond, and mom, Kitty, with me in Victory Lane after winning the Twin 125 at Daytona in 1983.

I had lost the previous two years right at the very end. Darrell Waltrip had beaten me both in 1981 and '82 right at the end of the season. Here he was breathing down my neck again, and we went to Riverside.

Riverside was one of my favorite places. We were out there, we started the race, and I had a flat tire. It was kind of a mystery, because there wasn't any trash on the track or anything. That tire tore up pretty bad; I got in and had it taken off, but lost a lap.

I had to finish within nine spots of Darrell Waltrip or lose the championship. Now,

Me and my NASCAR Winston Cup Series championship trophy at the Waldorf in 1983.

I was a lap down and he was running up front, not leading, but close to the front. There were 35 spots between him and me. So I'm a long ways away from where I need to be.

I was racing really hard and had a stroke of good luck. I was a lap down and behind Benny Parsons, who was leading the race, and the caution came out. In those days, we raced back to the caution anyways, and Benny hesitated for a split second and I got by him and got my lap back.

So I went around and pitted for gas and tires. About 10 laps after the restart, I ran out of fuel pressure. I said, "Wow, wait a minute. The guys didn't get the car filled with gas." So I radioed them and told them I was out of gas. Gary Nelson (crew chief) told me I had plenty of gas and to keep going. I told Gary we were in trouble because we had no fuel pressure.

He told me to keep on going; we had plenty of gas and not to stop. I told him we had to stop. So we stopped and they put more gas in. We'd run a few laps and then it would go to missing and carrying on again. So we had virtually lost this championship, as we were back in the 20th spot and struggling.

The 1983 NASCAR Winston Cup Series championship team.

Darrell Waltrip was up front and looking pretty good. Somehow, he got together with Tim Richmond, and Tim ran him off the race track and Darrell went for a big slide and I won the championship.

Here we were, trying to go to Victory Lane, and it's raining like the devil. We were really trying to have a good time. But I was really concerned as to why the car went to running bad and what happened.

Gary said that we won the championship, forget it. Well, I couldn't forget it. It took me two weeks to get them to look at that car. When they did, they found a 10 pound sack of sugar in the gas tank. It doesn't dissolve in a gas tank, it's like sand and goes in and stops everything up, and the filter was stopped up with sugar.

It was one of those bittersweet things.

My Favorite Victories

Whenever I'm asked about favorite wins, I always think of my very first 500-mile win, which was at Rockingham in 1967. I went down there with Holman-Moody for the very first time with Fred Lorenzen as the crew chief on the car.

He was a sight, but he really taught me about fine-tuning a chassis for late in the race. He could really work on that adjustment with the idea of what the track was going to do and what he'd need. When it seemed wrong early in the race, it was really going to be the right setup by late in the race.

We were able to win that first 500-miler and it was just a great event for me.

Winning at Charlotte several times was great, and Dover was great several times. Several other wins were really good, but the 1978 Daytona 500 was neat with Bud Moore. To come back from the wreck on Friday and win there was great. The 1982 Daytona 500 was pretty neat, getting the bumper knocked off after Joe Gazaway made us move it on Saturday.

The 1988 Daytona 500 should be my all-time favorite. To win the Super Bowl, at age 50, for the third time in your career, with the best young man in racing second to you—and have it be your son, Davey—would have to be the greatest victory in anyone's career.

But I still don't remember it. The crash at Pocono and the head injury took that memory away.

Here I am giving Davey a Miller beer bath after winning the Daytona 500 in 1988—the greatest race of my career. Davey finished second to me that day.

There's just a lot of great wins.

Bobby was involved in a first-lap crash at Pocono Raceway on June 19, 1988, in which he suffered career-ending injuries. After a lengthy recovery and physical rehabilitation, the only lingering effect has been a loss of memory regarding the early part of 1988.

The fans certainly had a good time back in the day—and they still do today.
That's my cardboard stand in "helping" them at a race.

The Legacy of Bobby Allison

As the time drew near and the realization dawned that all the storylines had been fulfilled that were sketched out, Bobby was asked one simple question.

"How do you want to be remembered 100 years from now, when they look at the record books, watch footage of NASCAR races and see your name prominently displayed?"

Y ou know, that's a really good question for me.

On the serious side, 100 years from now I would like for them to say, "There was a guy who contributed, heavily, to the popularity of this sport. It was a pretty young sport when he started. It wasn't brand new, but it was still pretty young.

"He worked hard, put his own earnings back into it and contributed heavily to the great success that it became."

On the fun side of things, somebody could say, "There's a guy, if ever he had all his stuff together at one time,

Just taking a little break at the race track in 1983.

would have been way, way ahead of where he was."

A long time from now, when people are looking at this whole picture, I just really hope they call me *A Racer's Racer.*

A very proud day for me. Here I am getting inducted into the International Motorsports Hall of Fame in 1993.

Thanks for the Memories!

Above: The best way to get Judy to Victory Lane was for me to stop and pick her up on pit road. Here we are after winning at Richmond in 1983. The nose on this Chevrolet was built in one week by me and some guys in my shop in Hueytown, Alabama. It beat everything in existence at the wind tunnel.

Above: I was king for a day in 1974 at Old Dominion Speedway in Manassas, Virginia. Frank Plesinger owned this car (No. 21).

Right: Here's Neil Bonnett, Donnie Allison and me "horsing around" on the infield of Charlotte in 1982.

Left: Judy and me in Victory Lane at Middle Georgia Raceway in 1967. That's Clifford over my shoulder and Davey above our heads.

Below: In Victory Lane at the 1982 Daytona 500 with my mom and dad.

Left: Vice President George Bush and me at the NASCAR Awards Ceremony in New York City. This was the year I won the championship in 1983.

Above: By this picture in 1990, you can see how much I sometimes enjoyed being a team owner.

Above: Apparently, I'm making Davey, Ned Jarrett, and everyone else laugh about something a Talladega in 1987.

Above: This was my first real team in 1972. We were one of the first teams to have a non-manufacturer sponsor—Coca-Cola in our case—on the car. Note the uniform pants on the crew.

Above: Here's the family, with Miss Union to the left, in 1969. I'm holding Carrie, in front f me is Bonnie, Davey, and Clifford, with Judy and her bouffant hairdo on the right.

Above: Here's Cale Yarborough, James Hylton and me "horsing around" at Dover Downs in 1980. That's me winning.

Above: Here is Donnie (right) and me with Melvin Joseph, the designer and builder of Dover, at Dover in 1973. Melvin is still a good friend today.

Above: Here I am being interviewed by Bob Myers (striped shirt) and signing autographs in 1971.

Above: I would help out Davey whenever I could by doing some hot laps in his cars. This was his No. 23 NASCAR Busch Series car in 1984.

Above: Bill France, Sr. and me discussing something that made us both smile in 1973.

Below: Here I am presenting President Ronald Regan with a Quaker State jacket in the garage at Daytona in 1984. This was the race where Richard Petty notched his 200th victory.

Left: This was me catching my breath after I won the Southern 500 at Darlington in 1983. That's Bill Broderick, known as the Hat Man, sitting next to me as I sip on a Miller High Life.

This is my Aerostar 700p that I landed on the backstretch of Daytona in 1984 the Wednesday before the 500-mile race. We hid this off the track back there under tarps. When I won the Twin 125 on Thursday, they "delivered" it to me just outside of Victory Lane. Three hours later, I took off from the backstretch of the track.

Bobby Allison's Career Achievements (1961-1988)

Accomplishments

NASCAR Winston Cup Series champion	1983 (Second in points four times)
NMPA Driver of the Year	1971, '72, '83
American Driver of the Year	1972, '83
Most Popular Driver	1971, '72, '73, '81, '82, '83
Career starts	717
Career victories	85 (84 according to NASCAR)
Top five finishes	331
Top 10 finishes	440
Poles	57
Best season	1972—10 wins, 12 second place finishes, 11 poles (five consecutively)
Daytona 500 wins	3 (1978, '82, '88)
Daytona sweep	1 (1988)

Named one of NASCAR's 50 Greatest Drivers in 1998
Founding member of famed "Alabama Gang"
Member of International Motorsports Hall of Fame
Member of North Carolina Motorsports Hall of Fame

Records

Oldest winner of Daytona 500	1988 at age 50
Most Superspeedway wins in one year	7 (1972), 5 ('78), and 7 ('82)
Most Consecutive poles	5 (1972)
Most Consecutive wins in a season	3 (1972, '83)
Career wins by brothers	94 (according to NASCAR)—Bobby (84), Donnie (10)
Tied or holds record for most wins at following tracks	Charlotte, Dover, and Riverside (Inactive)